Contents

LET'S HAVE IT OUT

THE BARE-BONES MANUAL OF FAIR FIGHTING

ARTHUR S. HOUGH, Ph.D.

CompCare® Publishers
2415 Annapolis Lane, Minneapolis, MN 55441

Library of Congress Cataloging Publication Data
Hough, Arthur S., 1928—
Let's have it out : the bare bones manual of fair fighting /
Arthur S. Hough.
p. cm.
ISBN 0-89638-237-0
1. Fighting (Psychology). 2. Conflict (Psychology).
3. Interpersonal conflict. 4. Anger. I. Title.
BF575.F5H68 1991
154.2'4—dc20   90-21929
                                                      CIP
Cover and interior design by Lois Stanfield
Originally edited by Betty Gardiner

Inquiries, orders, and catalog requests should be addressed to:
CompCare Publishers
2415 Annapolis Lane
Minneapolis, Minnesota 55441
Call toll free 800/328-3330
(Minnesota residents 612/559-4800)

6   5   4   3   2   1
96 95 94 93 92 91

Acknowledgments

Although I like to think of myself as a creator, after twenty years of developing the fair-fight method, I am actually more an innovator, expanding upon the excellent original work of the psychologist, Dr. George Bach, who, along with his staff, introduced fair fighting to me in workshops and texts. I owe Dr. Bach for such insights as ambush and appointment, placement of feedback, specificity of issues, crazymakers (foul ploys), and the attitudes necessary for effective fair fighting. Bach was a tough, perceptive teacher, and a pioneer in more than one breakthrough in interpersonal communication.

I would also like to credit Dr. Thomas Gordon for his enormous contribution to resolving human conflict in his clear theory that "he who has the feelings has the problem," a keystone of conflict resolution.

On the more personal side, you should know that although this is the first commercial edition of *Let's Have It Out,* I have published two previous versions for my students in integrative communication at San Francisco State University. I am indebted to their excellent feedback, and to my friend and roving amanuensis, Betty Gardiner, who edited and published these earlier editions.

NOTE TO THE CONFRONTED PERSON

When somebody says to you, "Let's have it out!" don't panic. No one is trying to box you in. Fair-chair fighting is designed to protect you as well as the person confronting you.

You are not being put at a disadvantage. You or your partner may be holding in things that ought to be dealt with, or perhaps your fighting creates more problems than it solves.

If your partner is doing it right when he or she starts a fair-chair fight, you are not being attacked. Your partner is inviting you into an arena in which your own needs and feelings are as important, but not more so, than his or hers. If your partner is not doing it right, then read through the simple rules of fair fighting with me and learn how to point out to your partner when you feel you're not getting a fair deal.

If there are rights or privileges or a special authority that you feel are yours, then say so and explain how you feel about them. Your needs and rights are important.

If you're the boss and have to take the responsibility or punishment for concessions you make to your subordinate, it is legitimate to have this out.

If you're the wife and you feel you're making all of the decisions about how to bring up the kids, then make this point.

If you're the teenage son or daughter in the family and you

believe that growing up means being allowed to make your own mistakes, make this part of your case.

If you're uncomfortable talking about your feelings and think that fair-fighting is a device to open you up, relax. Fair fighting means that your needs are respected. Speak your feelings as much or as little as you want to, but be willing to listen if your partner has feelings he or she wants to share.

WHAT HAPPENS WHEN WE FIGHT?

People have three options when it comes to fighting with each other: to fight dirty and hurt each other; to fight clean and win together; or to avoid fighting at all. Most of us don't fight at all because the only way we know is dirty fighting, and we're too nice for that. We could all fight constructively rather than destructively if we only knew how, but we don't. So, we grin and bear it, and say, "Oh, let it go." Why? Because this is what we think about fighting:

1. I'm going to lose and get hurt.

2. I'm going to win and be sabotaged down the line for it.

3. I'm going to say too much, hurt somebody, and feel guilty.

4. I'll bungle it somehow, and my partner will just draw away from me, and nothing will be solved.

We know that even when we fight and win, we lose, and that's too bad because with a few small changes in our attitude and our procedures, we could have it all. There is a clean and fair way to fight, and you can win at it because when you do it right, there are no losers.

NO LOSERS

Our overwhelming temptation in any fight is to force our partners to feel that they have lost. We then feel a false sort of triumph. But these encounters have few rewards. You may have won the fight, but you have lost in your relationship.
Nobody wants to lose, neither you nor your partner. But if both partners are going to win, they have to learn how to fight fair. Fair fighting is a special process in which partners negotiate to maintain a good relationship or improve a painful one. Your partner is anyone you are trying to fight with fairly.

If you want a fair fight in which you both win then you must look inside and ask yourself these five questions:

1. Do I want to hurt, injure, or put down this person?

2. Do I want to win over this person?

3. Do I want to establish who's right and who's wrong?

4. Do I want to make this person feel guilty?

5. Do I want to unload bad feelings from the past on this person?

These are tough questions. If you feel like saying "Yes!" to any of the first five questions, you'll go on holding in the pain and anger, suffering the actions of many people who don't even know they're hurting you, or fighting dirty and losing even when you win. Don't feel guilty about it; we've all been there plenty of times and will surely be there again. There are times when we are so angry, resentful, or hurt that we also want to hurt someone, score a few points, make our partners feel wrong and guilty, or just tell others how bad they've been to us.

The main question is: can you handle the problem without damaging your relationship? Try asking yourself the question below and see if your thinking begins to change.

Do I want to get rid of my present bad feelings about this person, remove the obstacle to our friendship or love, and change the relationship enough to feel closer to him or her than I feel right now?

As you think over your answer, you may find your reasons for saying "yes" to the first five questions dissolving. You can't improve a relationship by hurting someone, and improving a relationship is the purpose of this book.

WE NEVER FIGHT

You hear it at twenty-fifth wedding anniversary parties. "We never fight." They say it with great pride.

"We never fight" always implies "we never disagree," and this can't be true. Everyone disagrees, and when people live intimately together for years, those disagreements, when unconfronted, mean that someone has learned to accommodate. Accommodating can be many things: knuckling under to someone's wishes; manipulating people without their knowing it; repressing frustration and anger at your own expense; or taking your anger out on someone else.

"We never fight" really means, "we don't dare fight, for we would surely hurt each other if we did." People who love each other and fight don't need to be alarmed. Fighting often reveals deep needs that can't come out any other way. Fighting can also lead to intimacy and better understanding because compromises are more openly arrived at.

5

But an even greater use for fighting between couples is that a fight can be a good test of their love. One partner is saying to the other, "Do you really love me? Can you love me after seeing me angry, sulky, childish, irrational, and attacking?" If so, then the partners' love emerges more secure, not less so.

Think of how insecure untested love is to people with a normal sprinkling of self-doubt. If you have a partner with whom you've never fought, what evidence have you that the first fight or the second or the third will not crush or scar your relationship? So you have a choice: go ahead and test, using the most primitive tools of fighting, the destructive devices, or swallow the bad feelings and wait.

When you fight fairly, however, this love-testing can end. You learn to uncover each other's deeper needs and spot your partner's frustration early. Testing becomes unnecessary. You learn how to help rather than block an angry partner, or you may rechoose your feelings and step around a problem altogether.

Constantly accommodating, or giving way to a partner, is not a contribution to the relationship—it is an obstacle because it stifles the wholeness and health of one partner. The gift of accommodation becomes a burden of unspoken needs.

If you think your spouse or child won't love you if you disagree, or that your boss will punish you if you disagree, you are applying a fragile cover-up on a necessary, but troubled, relationship. Both partners, not just one, must grow, or the offended one seethes in silent anger or goes numb. This is no gift to either partner.

FAIR FIGHTING AT WORK

One-third of our adult lives is spent at work. Whatever we have chosen for our work has an enormous impact on our lives: it becomes up to one-half of all the influence we will ever have on the world, and one-half of the influence that the world will have on us.

Conflict at work can have terrible consequences. It can eat away at your joy of life. Any situation at work that makes you unhappy, causes you pain, or dulls your existence demands your immediate attention.

When asked what bothers them about their job, workers most commonly complain about their inability to get along with the boss and the feeling of being trapped in an unsatisfying job. Bosses make the same complaints. Bosses and employees can improve or eliminate their unhappy work environments by using fair-chair fighting.

So, it's time to face conflict and have it out—cleanly, fairly, and openly—for the good of your whole life.

WHAT'S FAIR ABOUT FIGHTING?

We've got lots more options than fair fighting, between silent suffering and dirty fighting. Fair fighting is a special-purpose process in which partners negotiate more appropriate behavior to maintain a good relationship or improve a painful one. Here are some of the most common options, each used to accomplish a slightly different end:

Argument: a disagreement in which logic and facts are used to prove and disprove a point.

Debate: an argument that follows formal rules of proof and evidence.

Dispute: an angry exchange of contradictory statements.

Controversy: a lengthy disagreement over a matter of some importance.

Quarrel: a disagreement marked by anger and deep resentment (also a wrangle, altercation, squabble, or spat).

Some disputes are one-sided—one partner does all the talking, lecturing, chastising, criticizing, reprehending, blaming, condemning, remonstrating, scolding, or putting down. If you are the partner who does all of the talking, you must also take the consequences. Your partner may respond with fear, guilt, hostility, resentment, and stubborn opposition.

FAIR FIGHTING AS FRIENDLY COMPLAINT

We often think of a disagreement as a war. We even use the vocabulary of war to describe a disagreement. We speak of adversaries, opponents, conflicts, strategies, and tactics. We say that people "have positions" like armies; they attack, counterattack, defend, maneuver, and retreat. There are stalemates, truces, surrenders, and victories. It's all very dramatic and emotionally exciting, except that in the aftermath of verbal warfare, people get hurt and relationships die, just as in war.

Fair fighting, on the other hand, when used early enough, resembles a friendly complaint rather than an attack and counterattack. It is persistent, peaceful negotiation, not war. To fight constructively, we must change the way we think of disagreements and eliminate the war-like vocabulary we use to describe them.

Constant accommodation, or giving way to a partner, is less a contribution to the relationship than it is an impediment, for it stifles the wholeness and health of one partner and thereby lessens, by crippling one partner's potential, the very gift that this accommodation is intended to be.

To think, "She won't love me if I disagree," or "He will punish me if I disagree" is to apply a fragile cover-up on an important relationship. Both partners, not just one, must grow, or the offended one either seethes in silent anger or goes numb.

VERBALIZING SOCIAL CONTRACTS

Every day we face a maze of unspoken contracts. There are accepted codes of behavior for spouses, teachers and students, bosses, teammates, partners, coworkers, and customers. Few of these rules are actually spelled out, and we all assume our partners understand the contracts they have with us. But these silent assumptions often break down. It can be as simple as who pays the check, who washes the dishes, who keeps a secret, or who initiates sex. Since most of our assumptions are unspoken, we all hope that our partners know the rules and are playing by them. When they don't, we feel cheated, hurt, and angry.

We make silent assumptions in almost any situation: a son comes back to live at home after years of college; a twenty-one-year-old daughter suddenly gets a new stepfather; a building contractor has to work with an architectural engineer; a man and a woman of different backgrounds decide to marry; a boss hires a new employee—all of these people have separate expectations. But normal communication channels become burdened by so many signals. There must be a clear channel for easy, nonthreatening negotiation.

Fair fighting becomes the channel for verbalizing and aligning interpersonal contracts. It brings those unspoken expectations into the open. A partner who suspects that he or she and a partner are making silent assumptions can say, "Here's how I see things. Here's what I need to have happen. How much of this would you agree to? Is there something I can do that would make this easier for you? Can we call this an agreement now?" They then make a verbal contract in which both partners fully understand the terms. The contract remains negotiable so the partners can honor each other's backgrounds, needs, and potentials.

You've already guessed what has to happen to benefit from healthy fighting. You both have to win. But everything has to be settled as well. Bad feelings have to be said and heard. Needs have to be laid out openly, and enough change has to occur for the bad feelings (on both sides) to dissolve.

THE BASIC PREMISE: A FAIR AND CARING PARTNER

THE CARE PREMISE

In fully functioning fair-chair fighting, both partners must care about each other. You must focus on the basic problem, which is that you have developed painful negative feelings that you want to get rid of—the argument is not about who is right and who is wrong. If your partner doesn't want to accept any responsibility for helping you get rid of your negative feelings, then you have a less-than-ideal partner.

For example, when one partner says, "I suffer from your smoke," the smoking partner should care that the nonsmoker is in pain. The smoker needs to be willing to give, but so does the complaining partner.

Two caring partners are, in effect, saying to each other:

I'm important; my needs are important.

You're important; your needs are important.

But not all of the people we want to get along with are going to care about us in return. Don't think of fair-chair fighting as something to try on a police officer giving you a ticket, or a county planning commission rezoning your neighborhood. They don't have to care about our bad feelings—they simply have to do their jobs. The new boss, the neighbor, the waiter in a restaurant do not need to care about us and never promised they would. When we face an uncaring person, we can fall back on the fair premise.

THE FAIR PREMISE

The fair premise says that other people want to be fair whether they care for you personally or not. We are brought up to care in general about other people's needs, and fairness often becomes a part of our self-image. While most people want to be fair, some don't. The sooner you know which partners are frequently unfair, the faster you can try the two strategies below.

Strategy One

Avoid attacking. You can raise or lower a person's fairness level by the way you treat that person. If you attack someone's self-image, you fault that person, and you may very well trigger feelings of defensiveness or guilt in your partner for having caused your pain. Now the argument is no longer about your needs, but about your partner's ego or self-image. Your partner will care much less about your needs than about his or her self-image.

If you want to preserve, maintain, or create caring or fairness in others, don't fault them. What your partner is doing is legitimate in terms of his or her needs until you successfully place your own needs against them. Don't confront the *right* or *wrong* of it; that's arguing, not fair fighting.

Strategy Two

Base the fight on a mutual need. A boss needs a subordinate to be loyal and reliable. A subordinate needs to get along with the boss. Parents need to raise their children successfully. Two work partners assigned to the same office need to be free of strife and hassle with each other so they can get their work done. These aren't just amenities; these are necessities. It is part of the job to get along and therefore to care about what's happening to the other people involved and to be fair about it. You won't meet many people immune to this argument when you put it properly.

THE UNCARING, UNFAIR, UNAWARE PARTNER

Sometimes you run into an uncaring, unfair, and highly defensive partner. You can also be pretty sure that this partner either doesn't know or has rejected the fair-chair process—an unaware partner.

You, the fair fighting partner, can alter your partner's basic position. If he or she fights dirty and you fight back, your partner will become even less flexible and more righteously entrenched in his or her bad habits of dirty fighting. However, if you respond with consistent fair fighting, persistently absorbing counterattacks with constructive confrontation, you can upgrade unfair to fair, uncaring to caring, and unaware to aware. (See Upgrading Poor Partners, pp. 75–82.)

Some conflicts may be beyond your skill or willingness to turn into fair fights. The partner could be a parent, mate, child, or work partner. Learning that your partner doesn't care about your pain, and being sure of it, is a very important discovery. The caring between you and your partner is more vital to your relationship than any argument at hand. If your partner turns away from caring about you and the relationship, then you will have to face the following steps with your partner:

1. I have these bad feelings, which I am creating but you are stimulating.

2. I have told you my needs and asked for help.

3. You are leaving me in this pain, and I have no other reasonable conclusion than to believe that it is because you don't care.

4. Now I have two problems: the one I started with and the larger one that you don't care about my pain or my need to remove the barriers between us.

5. Therefore, I must face most urgently the larger problem: Do we care enough about each other to maintain this relationship on a negotiating level? If not, then I must judge whether or not it is healthy for me to continue this relationship with you.

There may be times when you feel you can't leave a relationship because your needs or obligations are too strong: "I need this job," or "I won't leave my children."

Making the best of an uncomfortable relationship does not mean enduring pain or becoming a zombie with no feelings. Be aware, show you care, and have it out when necessary. Persist until your partner gets the message that pain, anger, and frustration have to be confronted and dissolved.

The basic premise for creating desired change rests, then, on a specific and general caring between partners, a sense of fairness as a principle of life, and a requirement that each person's self-image not be attacked.

HOW NOT TO FIGHT AT ALL

Not every partner is ideal. Some people choose to be unfair and uncaring. But be careful. An uncaring, unfair partner is not your immediate license to switch to dirty fighting. There are other options, some of them preferable to going dirty; others are painful options, and you must consider them carefully before choosing them.

ACCOMMODATING

Accommodating is the most frequent response to an unfair, uncaring partner. Many people take this position before they learn how to fight fair. To avoid destructive fighting, most people suppress their pain. They keep silent. They become martyrs. But by internalizing their own pain, they thwart their own human potential—they settle for less. And they allow the pain to roam around inside of them instead of getting it out in the open. These people become saboteurs because their pain is an energy that will make itself felt somewhere.

Here are some of the ways people use their pain for sabotage:

1. They sabotage themselves internally, resulting in headaches, indigestion, ulcers, high blood pressure, colonic

disorders, hypertension, and other illnesses caused by anger and stress.

2. They redirect their frustration by attacking and being generally unpleasant to other people who are not at fault.

3. They close down and withdraw, showing neither negative nor positive emotions. They become less loving.

4. They manipulate the person who is the source of their pain, using tricks, ploys, and devices to change their partner's behavior.

5. They learn to feel guilty for their own needs and condemn themselves for being so demanding and critical of their partner.

6. They find subtle ways to hurt their partner by allowing the partner to get into trouble they could have prevented. They might shun, ignore, or go around their partner. They stop laughing at their partner's jokes, or they follow orders to the letter, knowing that this is not what the other wants. They complain to others and give their partner a bad name. (You probably know the game and could continue this list.)

RECHOOSING

While accommodating is an unhealthy process because it stifles and submerges negative feelings (sometimes for years), rechoosing is the healthy internal alternative.

In any bad situation we have two separate reactions: the external and the internal. Externally, when someone causes us pain, we may either try to avoid the physical circumstances that cause our discomfort, or confront the partner and request a change.

Internally, we remain in charge of our feelings and can rechoose them. No person actually causes our bad feelings, but someone may stimulate us to react with those feelings. By accommodating, we hold on to the bad feelings and try to control them. By rechoosing, we change our reaction to the emotion and choose not to be frustrated, angry, disappointed, annoyed, or hurt. This is not suppressing the emotion, but dissolving it. Instead of saying, "I am controlling my anger," we say, "I am choosing not to react with anger."

An extreme example of rechoosing is an ex-con who was asked how long he had spent in prison. "Not a single day," he answered. "They controlled the body, but I controlled the mind."

To allow a partner to put you in pain is to consent to his triggering your automatic and historic categories. For example, the automatic/historic/categorical response to insult is anger or hurt. You give the partner this power, and you can also take it back. You say, in this instance, "I can be unthreatened by this insult, unangry and unhurt, and that's what I choose to be."

Some choices are harder than others. When it is easy to forgive a partner's actions, you can do it internally. When it is harder, you ask (externally) for change. If that fails, you still have the option of going back inside and choosing not to react emotionally. This can be difficult, but it's better than blowing up.

POWER PLAY

Each of us has some kind of power over our partners. When cornered, we are inclined to use it, either as a negotiating tool or as pure punishment. Here are some of the ways we use our power:

1. We withhold something from our partner: sex, money, privileges, good services.

2. We order, threaten, and warn, even to the point of violence.

3. We appeal to a higher authority by complaining to the boss, initiating a formal grievance procedure, calling in a "heavy" who has power over our partner, or taking our partner to court.

The power play usually brings on more conflict or withdrawal, but it is common among partners who cannot or will not fight and feel they have exhausted all of their other options.

GETTING HELP

Partners who want to save their relationships may decide together to seek outside help. There is a variety of trained people available for arbitration, counseling, and therapy. Sometimes you just need a friend who believes in fair fighting, knows how to use it, and can be fair to both partners.

Don't stop fair fighting when you start seeing a counselor. Counseling and therapy can stimulate fair fighting. When two people need to fight a lot, they might be missing what's really wrong. A good, analytically trained counselor can help them see the underlying issues.

GETTING OUT

There are bad relationships in which the cure is not worth the effort. Fair fighting tends to flush these bad relationships out into the open. If you have made the best efforts to heal a partnership in which you and your partner are constantly reacting to each other with pain, then you are faced with the realization that this is not how you intend to live your short life. You might decide that you must make a serious change. Quit the job. File for divorce. Move away. Leave.

I consider these options to be generally unnecessary and full of pain. Still, they are options. In each case, the basic theme is that you are not a captive of life or any of its relationships. But every choice has its consequences. Weigh them and decide.

Caring, trying to be fair, and negotiating without getting defensive are the three foundation stones of constructive confrontation. The process of fair fighting alone can bring out the care-fair-aware qualities in your partner. And fair fighting can nurture and develop these qualities where they are weak. There is really no effective substitute for fair fighting. It resolves, or it reveals.

BEFORE YOU FIGHT

Ideally, both partners in a fair-chair fight know what they are doing and why. They know the basic rules, and they are not fighting to win but to conduct a positive confrontation in a way that brings them closer together. But you cannot expect training in fair fighting from everyone you encounter, so you may want to introduce your partner to the fair fight chairs before a crisis arises. The worst way to approach your partner is to say, "I'm mad and I want to confront you fairly. Here are the rules." Already you have put him or her at a disadvantage. Below is my suggestion for introducing fair-chair fighting to your family, intimates, and close coworkers.

INTRODUCING FAIR FIGHTING TO A CLOSE PARTNER

Find a time with your partner (and this could be your whole family at once) when things are running smoothly. Tell your partner (or family) that you want to discuss something serious that you feel strongly about. Sit down in a place where you will not be distracted and present your case.

You will use your own words, but my personal script goes like this:

We love/like each other, and we don't want to hurt each other. But we do have differences—everybody does. I get peeved at you sometimes, and you get peeved at me. This is perfectly legitimate, but we should have a way to deal with those bad feelings without hurting each other or holding back our frustrations.

I've come across a method of airing problems and getting rid of bad feelings that should result in our loving each other even more, without blowing up, sulking, holding in, or feeling misunderstood.

Here it is: I've got a book on it. It has some simple rules for good fighting, and I'd like to try it. Will you read it so that the next time either of us has bad feelings we can sit down and work it out with both of us knowing what we're doing?

It's not just a game; it's easy to do, not complicated, and I'm serious about it. I want us to be happy together and happy as individuals as well. I need this. Will you give it a try?

Then be gently persistent. Bring it up again periodically and ask if your partner has read the book and would be ready to use it the next time something comes up.

But beware of one little pitfall: When people get interested in fair fighting, the first thing they often want to do is get rid of old or huge hurts, not current and manageable ones. ("You really embarrassed me last summer," or "I want to know where you really went on New Year's Eve, 1984.") There is a problem here, of course, and there may still be bad feelings, but with old hurts there is no opportunity for negotiation and change. Keep to current and specific issues.

Here's the bottom line of what you need to say in any way you say it best:

You are important and your needs are important, and I care. At the same time, I am important and my needs are important, and I need you to care about that, too.

APPROACHING ACQUAINTANCES AND STRANGERS

You can't go around making everyone you know read the book or follow the rules. Whenever you can get somebody to agree in advance that you will confront each other fairly, you are way ahead, but for everyone else, there is the principle of unilateral fairness.

Unilateral fairness simply means that *you* fight fair, and because you know the difference between fair and dirty fighting, you confront the dirty fighting of others as an issue in itself. You teach fair fighting by doing it. You also teach it by recognizing, identifying, and confronting dirty fighting. Unilateral fairness works for fights with distant acquaintances, such as more removed coworkers, people we meet in groups, and total strangers. I'll show you how to use it effectively in Stage 3, in the section on confronting your partner's ploys (pp. 49–59).

RULES TO PROTECT THE RELUCTANT

The biggest reason people don't like to fight is that they lose. Frequent winners are not so reluctant to confront, but losers wince at the very thought of making a scene. And we are all losers with one partner or another, simply because we are stronger with some partners and weaker with others.

Here are the worst of these fear-producing fighting tactics, and after each one is the antidote in fair fighting:

1. *Ambushes:* Fights often begin when one person forces a confrontation with someone who is off guard and not ready or able to fight. (See Hot Fights, pp. 28–29.)

   Antidote: Fair fights are by appointment only. The partner requesting the fight states the nature of the problem and the partners agree on a confrontation time.

2. *Vulnerability:* Everyone is afraid of being hurt, and each of us is vulnerable on some point. Some things we are willing to argue about; others we are not.

   Antidote: A partner can refuse to deal with some issues until he or she feels enough confidence to handle it in a fair fight.

3. *Fast Fights:* Most fights go too fast. We feel that we have to respond immediately and defensively. We react too quickly and say things bluntly and hurtfully. Also, in most relationships one partner is quicker and one is slower, one louder and one softer, one more rational and one more emotional. One partner is almost always less verbal or more introverted than the other. Partners quickly learn their own weaknesses and prefer not to fight at all when they know they will be overwhelmed or outmanipulated.

   Antidote: Feedback slows down most fights. One partner cannot answer a crucial point until demonstrating that he or she has heard the other partner accurately.

4. *The Win-Lose Expectation:* To fight in the usual ways means that you expect either to win or lose, and fights become frightening when you have to take that much risk.

Antidote: Your goal in fair fighting is to remove barriers and increase closeness, not to win and prove your partner is wrong. In fair fighting you explain your problem, state your feelings, listen to your partner's part of the problem and feelings, negotiate some change, and come to a resolution. Each wins something, and both win more respect and closeness.

You have two jobs to do before you engage in a fair fight:

1. Accept the goals of fair-chair fighting and learn how to do it.

2. Help your partner to do the same or, if that fails, use the principle of unilateral fairness.

DON'T POLICE YOUR PARTNER

Fair fighting is not a magic wand that touches people and makes them fair, caring, and aware all day long. Do not hold your partner to fair-chair fighting attitudes and rules at any other time than when you are sitting in the chairs. But do try to hold your partner and yourself to any agreements you made while in those chairs. Fair fighting is not a twenty-four hour service; it is an arena in time and space where people strive to be fair and caring. Eventually, fair fighting courtesies spread out into daily life. But don't be impatient and begin to police your partner's normal communication.

RIGHT AND WRONG

In fair fighting nobody tells you you're wrong for being where you are. Fair fighting is not about what's right and wrong. It's about people feeling unhappy over something and trying to make the changes and compromises necessary to feel good again. Your partner is making the point that he or she wants to feel better about you. Go with it, not against it.

The quickest way to take your equal place in fair fighting is to follow these simple guidelines:

1. Do a lot of listening.

2. Hold off your reactions until you really understand what's being said.

3. Don't worry about being defensive when you talk. Just say where you are.

4. Know that you are not being defined or classified—your partner simply wants to change some painful feelings to happy ones.

5. Don't accept a fight on a big issue just yet. You need to practice on smaller issues first. Ask your partner to stay simple and specific.

6. Read this book so that you are on an equal footing with your partner and can get some satisfaction out of clean fighting.

Yes, it's a risk. So is driving your car. But you learned how to drive, and now you get where you want to go. Give fair fighting the same chance.

STAGE 1
APPROACHING YOUR
PARTNER

ACTION

1. (Announcement) A says, "I've got a problem, a gripe, a beef, a peeve, a bone to pick with you."

2. B says, "OK, what's it about?"

3. A tells B the nature of the problem, but no details.

4. A and B make an appointment to hash it out.

COACHING

Risk. Fair fighting may be the best system yet devised among partners to heal wounds and settle gripes, beefs, and crises, but it is no free ride. There is no way to do it without feeling some risk, especially the first time with a partner.

It takes time to learn to trust the process. When you say to a partner, "I have a problem with you," your heart beats faster and anxiety threatens to cloud your mind. Your words, no matter how diplomatic, threaten another's self-image.

It takes a great deal of strength to initiate a fair fight. You know that you are taking a risk. Not only do you challenge your partner, but you make a commitment to fairness, which means that all of your own dirty fighting tactics are now illegal. You are both making someone else vulnerable and agreeing to be vulnerable yourself.

You come to the edge of the pool—you plunge—you surface and breathe. You begin to swim. You will not drown, but to know that you must take the plunge.

If you never confront your partner, you feel a false security, believing that "If I don't criticize you, then you will be out of line to criticize me." In fair fighting there is no false security. Both partners are equally entitled and equally vulnerable.

It may seem as though the initiator is less vulnerable than the confronted partner, but this is not true in fair-chair fighting. There are no prosecutors and no defendants. Often the confronted partner is just waiting for a chance to pour out his or her own gripes. Prepare yourself for feeling vulnerable and don't be surprised by it.

MAKING AN APPOINTMENT

It's quite simple, but setting an appointment time makes a world of difference. Already you have two negotiators working to accommodate themselves and each other equally.

A: I've got a problem with you that I want to talk about. Will you work with me on it?

B: Sure. What's it about?

A: It's about your being late for the Monday morning staff meeting.

Notice that the initiator states only the nature of the peeve. This is not the time to launch into an argument. The precise nature of the issue may affect an accused partner's need to gear up to the fair-fight process. Fighting about money, for example, may require more gearing-up time than fighting about the dinner schedule. Also, if there is to be a delay, it is cruel to keep your partner guessing about what the problem may be.

> *B:* Well, I've had two drinks and I don't want to fight right now. How about after the evening news?

> *A:* Thanks for such a short delay. We'll do it then.

Both partners must negotiate for an acceptable time for the fight. No partner may unilaterally choose the moment. That is an ambush, and ambushing is dirty fighting. Making an appointment emphasizes the equality between the partners and protects them both from sudden outbursts of temper.

When one partner feels stronger than the other, he or she feels safe to attack. One partner might start fights just before going to work, making use of a hit-and-run advantage. Bosses are notorious hit-and-run artists. Some partners start fights at bedtime, sometimes as a means of sexual blackmail and sometimes because they can hold their partner's sleep as hostage.

HOT FIGHTS

Why not fight at the very moment when you are angry? Doesn't it weaken your motivation and your willingness to speak honestly about emotions when you delay a fight by appointment?

No. Whether it makes you feel more aggressive or not, immediate anger threatens fair fighting. Hot, spontaneous fights do not generally lead to constructive resolution. For one thing, expressing anger while you are feeling angry nearly always makes you angrier. Your emotions are supercharged, and you have a strong desire to hurt, which is both unfair and dangerous.

Making an appointment tends to cool your anger. Once you have successfully arranged an appointment, you are able to say, "We are willing to talk about it. Things can change. My needs are not being ignored."

Put yourself in your partner's position. You are coming home from a party, and your spouse attacks without warning. Or you and your boss have left a meeting at work, and he or she launches an attack. It takes highly skilled and experienced partners to move instantly into a fair fighting stance under such conditions. Still, no partner should artificially delay a fight so long that the initiator is left holding on to smoldering negative (and now revealed) feelings.

Some couples institute a twenty-four hour rule, agreeing that no fight may be postponed longer than one day. Experienced partners shorten their delay time as they gain trust in the fair-fight process. Eventually, partners learn to allow a hot confrontation to begin immediately, or as soon as there is time and space for an uninterrupted encounter.

STAGE 2
STARTING A FAIR-CHAIR
FIGHT

ACTION

5. Sit in two facing chairs with no distractions around you. Schedule at least a half-hour free time.

6. A says, "Here's my problem, and here's how it makes me feel about you."

7. B feeds back that entire message, without adding anything, until A agrees that B has heard correctly.

8. B then counters by giving whatever response he or she thinks is appropriate.

9. A feeds back that entire message to B's satisfaction.

COACHING

Before the fight begins, think about why you're fighting. You may know what the issue of the fight is, but do you know what the fight is about? Remember, a fair-chair fight is about needs, not about right and wrong. You want to do what you feel you need to do, and you want to give your partner the same privilege. So what you are really focusing on is a conflict of needs, not opinions, personal principles, or evidence of how right you are.

WHOSE PROBLEM IS IT?

You don't ever ask for a fair-chair fight with your partner because he or she has a problem. You confront because *you* have one. But people get this all mixed up, so let's start at the top.

When a problem comes up, we are tempted to look outside of ourselves for the blame because we want to believe that the problem originated out there. We are inclined to think:

You have done something wrong.

You have caused me discomfort.

You shouldn't do that.

We tend to fall back on unspoken rules, laws, and principles, so that whoever breaks one of these codes is automatically wrong—and therefore censorable, because he or she has a problem.

But it's not our partner who has a problem. If your son keeps his room dirty, whose problem is it, his or yours? If your subordinate is coming in late every day, whose problem is it, the subordinate's or yours? Right or wrong, neither the son nor the late employee has a problem until you give him or her one.

The problem starts when you have negative feelings (of anger, disappointment, worry, frustration, guilt, resentment, hurt) toward your partner. Those feelings are yours, not your partner's. You have the original problem.

If your little girl plays too roughly with the puppy, she has no problem with it—you do. How foolish and inaccurate to speak to her as though she has a problem when you are the one with the feelings. She might be the stimulus to your feelings, but your feelings belong to you.

You don't have a problem because someone hurt you or made you angry, but because you actually chose the negative feelings (being hurt or angry) from among the other feelings you might have chosen instead. In the world of human emotion there is no preset stimulus and response as there is when you touch the leg of a frog with an electrode. We choose every emotion from our personal assortment of feelings. Some feelings are easier to choose than others because of our backgrounds, habits, and needs. When you insult me, it is harder for me to choose to be amused or curious than to choose to be hurt and angry, but I am still not a frog's leg. I am a human faced with complex choices.

Even when someone truly wants to hurt you, he or she can't without your cooperation. All your partner can do is aim at the button in you that can turn on the hurt. You have to be the one to push that button. *In fair fighting you always approach a partner by admitting that you have found it easy to be hurt or angry by something he or she has done, and you'd like some help in changing how you feel.*

However, it is hard for us to believe that we are the cause of all our problems with other people, so we think:

If you had not provided the stimulus, I wouldn't feel this bad. (True)

I would not have chosen to be hurt. (True)

You are at fault for forcing me to choose these bad feelings. (Not true)

YOU CAN'T DEFINE YOUR PARTNER

In personal relationships there is no objectivity. You cannot tell your partner what he or she is by objective standards. You have passed the definition point. A boss, a teacher, a parent, a coach, a judge can make a good case for being objective when he or she is speaking with the perspective of someone who is trained to teach and guide. They are leaning on the objective standards derived from their own training.

But when you or I speak to a partner about our relationship, we are always talking about our own personal feelings, expectations, and opinions, not some universally accepted reality about our partner. The most challengeable sentences you ever say to your partner start with the words "You are. . . ." Statements that begin with "I" are the only truth you can deliver when a relationship is at stake. For example:

I see you as . . .

I think you are being . . .

You come across to me as . . .

I feel that you don't . . .

You seem to me to be . . .

Being personal truths, these are unchallengeable statements. Partners can always object to and evade being defined by you, but they cannot reasonably deny that your own personal perceptions are how you see them. It is your relationship that you are always addressing, not your partner's definition in the objective world.

LEVELING VS. BLAMING

There are short-term advantages to accusing the world for your painful feelings: When you think others are to blame, you have less personal anxiety, you feel strong for bearing your burdens, and you can even forgive people and feel ennobled. Be careful that you are not evading responsibility for your own feelings to claim these rewards.

But you have this wonderful, reliable signal that the problem is really yours: the bad feelings. When the bad feelings are yours, the problem is yours to that degree because you could have chosen not to have those bad feelings.

All this makes an enormous difference in how you treat a partner in fair fighting. Your proper response to others is to level with them that you have allowed this negative feeling, not blame them for it. In fair fighting it all boils down to this:

I have negative feelings about you for something you do. They are my signal that I have a problem. I want to get rid of these feelings, but it's hard as long as you keep presenting me with this stimulus. Will you help me with this? Will you please change the stimulus to a more positive one?

But other people are not in this world merely to serve you, so we have an equation that satisfies both the person with the problem and the person who is its stimulus, and this is the basis of every fair-chair fight:

A.   I am important and my needs are important; therefore, my needs are legitimate. Please take them seriously.

B.   You are important and your needs are important; therefore your needs are legitimate. I will not ignore them.

C. Since our differences here are based on our mutual needs, a problem is only a problem when someone's needs aren't being met and he or she has bad feelings about it.

THE "WHO'S IMPORTANT?" SEESAW

Two people sit on opposite ends of a seesaw. They both sit comfortably erect with their feet on the ground. They are in equilibrium with each other, which fits many of our ideals of a fine relationship: equality, sharing, togetherness, fifty-fifty. They teeter-totter a little and enjoy the sensation of movement and change.

Then one wants to go high and see over the wall. The other must descend to the ground to get him there. Then she wants to see over the wall, and he comes down to support her rise. His needs are important and so are hers. If one gets greedy and wants to stay on top all of the time, the other must stay on the ground, and the relationship becomes unbalanced. A good seesaw requires constant movement.

Practical relationships are like seesaws because one partner, by common agreement, might be more important than the other at one moment, but not at the next. If both partners were always equally important, the seesaw would stay still with no movement or change.

As a partner, you sometimes get more than is fair, sometimes less. A sensitive person knows when he or she needs more and when to accept less for the good of the relationship, but this should be the product of open negotiation, not silent accommodation or secret manipulation. Expressing negative feelings keeps the seesaw in motion because the feelings indicate when one partner is sitting too long on the low side of the seesaw.

I'M NOT TELLING YOU ABOUT YOU—
I'M TELLING YOU ABOUT ME

In fair-chair fighting we take responsibility for our own needs, but we let go of our partner's needs. This is the attitude in fair-chair fighting:

> I can't take care of both of us in this situation.
>
> I can't tell you what you need or why.
>
> You're going to have to do that.

Start out with, "I am; I feel, I need," not "You are, you feel, you need." Talk about your own problem, not your partner's. (Don't be premature in pushing the needs of us in a fair-chair fight. Us is the sum of you and me. The concept of us is what emerges when you and I agree.)

The result of all this taking responsibility for your own needs and feelings is that you now tell your partner:

> *After hearing my problem, if you feel you can share it or recognize a problem of your own, it is your choice. I'm not trying to give you a problem, only to ask your help with mine.*

PROBLEM CONVERSION

Suppose you are convinced that someone else does have a problem, and you want that person to change, what you really want to say is:

You have a problem. You smoke too much.

or

You are terribly defensive. You alienate yourself from people.

Now you are not stating your own problem, but stepping into someone else's life, offering unasked-for criticism and therapy. If your partner has not thought of this behavior as a problem before, you are giving him or her a problem. The problem is no longer smoking or defensiveness, but you.

There is, of course, a more authentic and effective approach. If your partner smokes too much for you, your proper approach is to speak only of the degree to which his or her smoking gives you a problem. This is problem conversion, and here's how it works:

I have a problem. I'm worried about your health when you smoke so much, and even though you don't care that you can get sick and die from it, I do. I want you and need you healthy.

or

I have a problem. At times I hear so much defensiveness when you talk to me that I feel my needs are illegitimate to you and that you think everything I say is an attack. (Give a specific and recent example.) I back away from you when I really want to be a friend. And I am embarrassed and anxious when you attack other people.

Now you are admitting to your own part of the problem—you are not giving a problem to your partner or insisting that your partner has one. You are stating your own legitimate, negative feelings.

If your partner feels threatened by this, emphasize the point that you are only stating your own problems.

Most partners respond positively to this—out of relief that for once someone is not telling them that they have a problem. Out of fairness or caring for you, they become more flexible—often to the point of admitting to their own part of the problem:

You're right. And it's really my problem we're talking about. I'm willing to discuss how I might deal with it.

Each partner sticks to his or her own problem until the other asks for help.

SPEAKING YOUR FEELINGS

Talking about feelings is something we have trouble doing without embarrassment, especially when it comes to negative feelings. Here are ways to make talking about your bad feelings easier:

1. *Don't Hold on to Feelings until They Build Up.* Don't wait, as you may have done in the past, until the bad feelings are so strong that they burst out in a mushroom cloud. Confront early.

2. *Reveal Feelings as You Feel Them.* Once your partner knows that you are generating bad feelings, he or she is likely to reduce the stimulus, and your bad feelings won't escalate. Expressing yourself doesn't mean that you go around all day saying how you feel, but that you use the fair chairs when you begin to feel pain.

3. *Find the Right Words for Your Feelings.* Find the name for how you're feeling. Don't just say, "I'm mad," if you can be more precise. There are a dozen levels to being mad. (See lists of specific feelings, pp. 104–106.)

4. *Don't Overstate Your Feelings.* We often overstate our bad feelings and use them like a battering ram on our partner. Or we exaggerate simply to get our partner's attention. In fair-chair fighting the whole purpose is to pay close and sincere attention to our feelings, which makes overstating unnecessary.

5. *Don't Understate Your Feelings.* Don't sell your feelings short by understating them. Don't say "Perhaps, maybe, I seem to be— angry," or "I have a tendency to be upset when you do such and such," or "I'm a teeny bit miffed at you" in order to be nice. Your partner is expecting and deserves your honesty. Say it like it is.

ESTABLISHING THE MENTAL SET AND PHYSICAL SETTING

It's very important to start a fair fight with the right attitude and in the right atmosphere. Here are the ground rules for sitting down in the fair chairs:

1. Make sure both partners have scheduled enough time. Though many fights take only five minutes, you should reserve at least a half-hour.

2. Sit in two chairs facing each other. Don't try to fight in a car or with one partner in the living room and one in the kitchen. Don't fight in bed.

3. Get rid of distractions: telephones, children, observers, food cooking in the kitchen, interruptions from the office. There should be no one else around.

4. Establish a lock-in situation. Make an agreement that neither partner breaks off suddenly. Both partners must

agree on interrupting or ending the fight. ("Time-out" provisions are explained in Stage 3, p. 48–49.)

5.   Be sure to tell your partner how important this process is to you, if you have not yet made that point in all these preparations.

6.   Be specific. State a single, specific, current problem, not a vague dissatisfaction, and do not drag in past history. State clearly how you feel about the incident. Remember, separate stimulus from cause. He or she is the stimulus. Your reaction to this stimulus is the cause of your bad feelings.

VAGUE: "You have ignored me repeatedly lately."

SPECIFIC: "You left me at the party last night, and I felt ignored."

7.   Use "I" statements. Keep your statements centered around your feelings so you won't sound as if you're making accusations. Blaming statements will only alienate your partner.

BLAMING: "You make me feel worthless."

LEVELING: "When you ignored me, I felt worthless, and I still feel hurt."

8.   Keep it simple. Keep the actual issue as small as you can— a single incident, if possible, and certainly a recent one, fresh in the mind of your partner, is easy to get hold of. The sentence "You're always putting me down" is not a fair fight, it's guerilla warfare, and it covers an issue that's far too big for inexperienced fighters.

If you have trouble getting satisfaction from a small, specific issue, then try linking fights; that is, as a second or third or fourth issue surfaces, set it aside for a subsequent fight. As a beginning white belt fair-chair fighter, you are not yet ready for taking on big, complex issues. Keep using small issues until you and your partner are experienced and can use the Grouping method. (See the section on Black Belt Fighting, pp. 83-88.)

In fact, don't look condescendingly on fighting over trivia. It trains you, tests you, and keeps bad feelings from building into larger fights. Fighting over trivia is simultaneously a safe process and a safety valve. Trivia are the tiny tangibles of deep hurts, fears, and frustrations, and can carry as heavy a load of feelings as larger issues.

STAGE 3
NEGOTIATION

ACTION

10. A and B negotiate, feeding back to each other at all crucial points.

11. A and B stay locked in, keeping the following attitudes in mind:
    a. Maintain good faith.
    b. Stay authentic, realistic, involved, and good natured.
    c. Stay focused on the issue.
    d. Use feedback when necessary for crucial points.
    e. Introduce and negotiate demands of each other.
    f. Call a time-out if the need arises, and schedule the next meeting.
    g. Avoid foul ploys or confront them when they appear.

COACHING

Stage 3 is really the heart of the fight. While I have given you a structure to follow at both the beginning and the end of a fair-chair fight, the middle ground belongs to you. It must be spontaneous because you are following your own needs, not some prescribed format.

STATING DEMANDS

The initiator has already stated the problem and his or her feelings about it. The receiver has countered with first reactions, which may include justifications, countergripes, explanations, and even apologies.

The whole process in having a fair-chair fight is to create some change in behavior, perhaps for both partners. The next step in the negotiation stage is a request for change. The initiator should be ready at this point to say, "Here's what I want, or would like, you to do."

If you delay too long making this request and the argument begins to stall, your partner should ask, "What do you want of me? What do you want me to do that will make you feel better about this?"

THE FOUR BEST ATTITUDES

If there is anything that fair fighting aims at directly, it is maintaining a good attitude. Each partner must keep the quality of the engagement high. The actual level of the encounter goes up or down according to the personal attitudes that send out constant signals of the temperment, assumptions, and intentions of the partners.

Having watched hundreds of fair, and not so fair, fights in classes and workshops, I have narrowed down the list of essential attitudes for a fair fight to four:

1. *Authentic.* I am willing to be myself, with a minimum of my normal defenses, and not play roles by being nitpicky, lofty, cute, cynical, worldly, bulldoggish, or saccharine sweet.

2. *Realistic.* I am willing to keep my demands within the limits of my partner's abilities and temperament and am willing to consider reasonable changes in myself, acknowledge my own faults and weaknesses, and not be demanding or evasive.

3. *Involved.* I am willing to take this fight seriously, listen carefully, feed back honestly, and be vulnerable—and not be distant and casual.

   Partners should face each other squarely. Body language should be direct, open, and alert. Slouching, twisting, fiddling, tapping, and gazing off are physical signals that a partner may be avoiding the argument. Your tone of voice may be mocking or threatening to the partner.

4. *Good Natured.* I am willing to be here, and ready to see the light side when it comes—not be grim and intimidating.

   Fair fighting really can be funny, and good humor demonstrates the genuine goodwill of the partners. The occasional light touch, so long as it does not become an evasion of the real issues, breaks the tension in fair-chair fighting. It must, however, be joyous humor, not sarcasm, ridicule, or malicious teasing. These last are foul ploys that put down the partner and his or her needs.

STAYING FOCUSED

Beware of one thing leading to another. A fight that loses its focus spreads out like butter on a hot stove and cannot be easily shaped. Deal with the gripes and countergripes, but don't expand the problem, add to it, or dip into the past. When new issues appear, set them aside for later fights, but don't be distracted by them.

THE FALSE ISSUE

It is not unusual, in the initial phases of a fair fight, for one or both of the partners to realize that they have uncovered in their opening arguments a deeper, related, or completely new issue that should have priority. We don't always start with the real problem. It is best to recognize the bigger argument, postpone the lesser issue, and start fresh with the newly unearthed problem. This sudden switch can only happen fairly by mutual consent between partners.

FEEDBACK AND COUNTER

Both partners feed back what the other has said at every point in the fight where they feel it is needed, but especially at the beginning, at crucial points in the middle, and at the end. However, if you feed back every statement, the fight would never end. That is why, in the negotiation stage, you use it only for crucial statements.

Here's how you feed back: Answer your partner by restating what you just heard. Use your own words when possible. Try to avoid parroting back word for word. Leave nothing out and add nothing of your own. Avoid slipping in your own editorials. You may have to repeat and change your feedback a few times before your partner agrees that you have restated what he or she said. Do not answer your partner's statement until you can feed it back to his or her satisfaction. Your partner may help you in the feedback as long as he or she doesn't use this opportunity to add on to the original statement.

You can introduce feedback with any of these helpful phrases:

What you're telling me is . . .

I hear you saying . . .

You feel . . .

You want me to know that . . .

FEEDBACK AS MAGIC

One of the greatest gifts you can give to another person at any time is to listen deeply, hearing not just the content but the feelings as well. We can give this gift through accurate feedback. In a conflict situation, where both partners need desperately to be understood, good feedback, all by itself, enormously reduces the gap between them. It generates respect and reinforces their human dignity. Here's how it works:

1. *Feedback Slows Down the Fight.* It gives both partners a chance to locate their best answers, not their quick-trigger defenses.

2. *Feedback Separates Listening from Responding.* Our biggest fault in listening is that we are always responding, resisting, and distorting as we listen, which, in the privacy of our minds, helps us feel that we're winning. Feed-

back, on the other hand, forces us to quiet our inner noise long enough to register accurately what our partner actually said.

3. *Feedback Gives Importance to the Speaker.* When we argue before listening properly, our partner feels ignored or slighted. Our silence works the same way. Feedback recognizes the importance of both partners.

4. *Feedback Keeps the Fight Limited to the Issue.* Once a partner has stated a problem and the other has fed it back accurately, the issue is defined and the level is set. The initiator can't keep adding to it by saying, "And another thing. . . ." The listening partner should question any additions or changes the initiator tries to make.

5. *Feedback Keeps Partners from Hearing Only What They Want to Hear, or Can Easily Deny.* Feedback prevents the listener from exaggerating an argument or feeling. When a feedback partner says, "Well, you just don't like having me around!" or "You're calling me a liar!" the speaking partner can make an immediate correction.

6. *Feedback Cuts Down on Secondary Fights.* A popular short-circuiting device called the secondary fight does not deal with the issue, but rather with what the partner did or did not say about it. It sounds like this:

"You said . . . !"

"I never said that!"

"Yes, you did! I heard you!"

"No, I didn't!"

"You did!"

"I didn't!"

You can see how the actual issue can be derailed unless feedback is used early in the fight.

BREAK OFF

The worst breach of good faith, outside of violence itself, is for one partner to break off and leave the fight. When two people have worked hard to find good common ground, it is disastrous to break off the fight and leave. Both partners must begin again to build up their good faith.

TIME-OUTS

However, it is fair to call for a temporary time-out. No partner should feel like a prisoner to any communication process. Partners can get overloaded, either with the issue or with their own emotional response to it. If you realize that you are jamming up emotionally, simply say so, and request a little time to think and pull yourself together. It's only fair for your partner to agree to a break.

Overusing time-outs can become a foul ploy—manipulating a partner and avoiding the issue.

There are also unpredictable distractions and interruptions that may stop a confrontation. You might have to break off suddenly by mutual agreement. As soon as the interruption is over, you either go back to the chairs or make an appointment to resume the fight later. Every time-out should be accomplished by an agreement as to when the partners will resume the fight.

Hold your time-outs down to the following four circumstances:

1.   Emotional overload

2.   Undeniable interruption

3.   A need to seek more information (consulting a third person, for example)

4.   Time to allow a partner to process his or her own readiness to change (see Stage 4, pp. 60–66)

THE FOUL PLOY

The foul ploy is the wicked witch of fair fighting. It is dirty fighting, pure and simple, but it's also the only kind of fighting that most people know.

In fair-chair fighting, we confront these foul ploys. Dr. George Bach, the famous and skillful originator of fair fighting, calls these ploys the "crazymakers."[1]

A ploy is a maneuver intended to outwit or discomfort another person, and when we add foul to it, we describe what makes it such bad news in fair fighting. Foul means rotten, lazy, stinking, offensive, loathsome, tangled, snarled, against the rules, treacherous, dishonest, and unfair, either by accident or intention.

FOUL PLOYS VS. HURTFUL WORDS

You may not call a foul ploy every time your partner uses hurtful words or actions. Hurtful words are intrinsic to fighting,

---

1. Dr. George Bach and Peter Wyden, *The Intimate Enemy: How to Fight Fair in Love and Marriage* (New York: Wm. Morrow, 1969). Dr. George Bach and Dr. Herb Goldberg, *Creative Aggression: The Art of Assertive Living* (New York: Avon Books, 1975).

even fair fighting. When you sit in the fair chairs, you are not just ordering pizza.

To be a foul ploy, the tactic must have placed you at a disadvantage, reducing your ability to respond or maneuver, boxing you in, or channeling or controlling your responses. Many foul ploys are not directly hurtful at all—they are merely the cunning, artful work of a passive aggressor.

MOST POPULAR FOUL PLOYS

There are, unfortunately, hundreds of foul ploys. You will find new ones in almost every dirty fight. Some are blatant, some subtle.

The following ploys are merely a sample, listed mainly to help you identify a foul ploy when it arises. The labels are not important, but partners must be able to recognize an unfair manipulation when it appears. Often a fair-chair fight has to pause while the partners negotiate these foul ploys out of the fight.

1. *Land Mine.* A partner blows up and goes into a rage or rampage. One golden rule applies here: No one touches a Land Mine. Leave your raging partner alone. There is no civilized way to communicate with this person at this time. Do not mock the exploder with silence, just avoid an encounter.

2. *Crossfire.* Two partners blow up because the second didn't follow the golden rule of Land Mine: he or she hooked into the rage of the first partner. This is a double foul ploy. If it happens, partners must stop and cool off. There is no civilized alternative.

   However, there is a way to handle the level of anger that brings on a Land Mine or Crossfire with minimal bad consequences. Partners make a special agreement that each, for a limited time, may dump an irrational emotional load on the other without feedback or future reference to the things they say in their outbursts. (See Haircut and Backcut in the section on Black Belt Fighting, pp. 83–85.)

3. *The Attic.* Widening the argument by reaching back into the past. The initiator may not fatten the issue by adding past incidents, but a receiver may make limited references to the past when explaining the causes of his or her present actions.

4. *Multiple Listing.* Bringing up more than the original single problem. The initiator must not list several issues for argument. A receiver, however, may introduce a countergripe if it clearly interlocks with the original issue.

   For experienced partners, and only by special agreement, multiple incidents of the same problem may be introduced into a fight. This is called Grouping and is described in the Black Belt Fighting chapter.

5. *Overload.* Giving your partner too much to remember or feed back in any one exchange, going on and on in a monologue. Watch for telltale phrases such as, "And another thing. . . ."

6. *Break Off.* Getting up and leaving the chairs without prior agreement with the partner. Temporary time-outs, however, are legitimate when partners agree to them.

7. *Sarcasm.* Negative humor, either in spoken content or in physical manner, which is sarcastic, maliciously teasing, snide, or contains hurtful insinuation. This is the opposite of positive or joyous humor, when both partners can laugh.

8. *Psychiatry.* Making comments that refer to your part-
    ner's mental state (as in "You're being childish!") or
    offering psychological reasons for your partner's be-
    havior or motivation. ("Oh, you're just projecting when
    you say that.") Psychiatry also includes denying the le-
    gitimacy of a partner's feelings. ("Now you really aren't
    that upset, are you?")

9. *Guilting.* Trying to make your partner feel totally re-
    sponsible for your own bad feelings. Remember that
    although your partner might offer the stimulus for bad
    feelings, you chose those feelings. Such comments as
    "You have hurt me deeply," or "You made me do this"
    are placing false guilt on your partner. (See Whose
    Problem Is It? pp. 31–32.)

10. *Doghouse.* Dredging up your partner's previous sins
    that he or she has already admitted to and dealt with. We
    do this to make our partner look bad by showing how
    often he or she has been wrong in the past. Don't play
    "Here we go again!" on settled issues.

11. *Double Bind.* Setting up a "damned if you do and
    damned if you don't" dilemma for your partner, in
    which whatever answer he or she gives will be a wrong
    one. In this ploy, anything your partner says will be to
    his or her disadvantage.

12. *Interrogation.* Repeatedly questioning your partner,
    under the pretense of getting a better understanding of
    the problem. Your questions keep your partner on the
    defensive and save you from having to respond.

13. *Mea Culpa.* Bidding for sympathy or implying that you
    are being misused or misunderstood, without actually
    saying it. You accept guilt for everything, unqualified
    and undefended, in order to stop your partner from

criticizing you. This includes such crazymaking statements as "I'm just no good; I don't know how you can stand me. I'm no good to anyone."

14. *Crying/Sulking.* Looking for sympathy or implying that you are being misused and misunderstood without actually saying it. There is nothing wrong with crying, and sulking is easy to do when confronted, but don't substitute either of these devices for verbalizing your feelings. Crying and sulking are foul ploys only when they disrupt the dialogue.

15. *Silent Treatment.* Leaving a partner hanging, without feedback or response. Like an animal freezing before the hunter, in order not to reveal itself, the silent partner is using a method of escaping painful negotiation. If the silent one is really so emotionally overloaded that he or she finds it too difficult to respond, the partners should negotiate a time-out.

16. *Third Party.* Evading responsibility by laying it on a third party who is not present. A fair-chair fight bogs down instantly when there is a missing factor. For example:

A: But I told Ann to call you and tell you I'd be late.

B: She did call me, but she said nothing about your being late.

When you need to consult a third party, call a time-out until you can contact that person and supply the missing information.

17. *Parent.* Talking down to your partner, adopting a condescending parent-to-child tone, or maintaining superiority on some topic when none has been awarded. For example, if you reply to your partner's argument with "That's not important," you are implying that you know better than your partner what is or is not impor-

tant. You can legitimately say, without being challenged, "That's not important to me."

18. *That's the Way I Am.* Claiming that mysterious or uncontrollable forces inside you make you act the way you do. But this is false—no one is irretrievably the way he or she is. We all make choices about the way we are. Some of those choices are hard ones, but they are not automatic.

19. *Sick-Out and No Pity.* Using physical ailments as an escape from the responsibility, as in "You know how sick I get when. . . ." Watch out, also, for the no pity ploy, the opposite of sick-out, in which you say, "I don't want any special treatment just because of my disability. . . ," and then you later come up with, "You're really merciless, aren't you?" (Don't call it hypochondria; that word triggers other bad feelings that complicate the fight at hand.)

20. *Comparison.* Comparing your partner to somebody else or requesting that your partner be more like somebody else. For example, "Why can't you be more like . . . ," or "Why can't you be more patient and understanding?" If you need your partner to change, simply make that request. When you use the comparison ploy you are ridiculing your partner and sidetracking the issue.

21. *Classing.* Classing your partner with some stereotyped group, as in "I know about alcoholics; my father was one"; "You people are all alike"; or "You're a typical college-graduate boss." Classing dehumanizes your partner by ignoring his or her individuality.

22. *Gendering.* Accusing, excusing, or making demands of your partner for behavior that you think is common to

his or her sex, as in "that's just like a woman," or "I want a man who. . . ." This is a special form of classing, also known as the masculinity/femininity ploy. Gendering turns your partner into a mere object fulfilling a stereotypical role. You can express the same feelings or needs without referring to gender, such as "I want you to. . . ."

23. *Real World.* Implying that your partner doesn't live in the real world as you do and is too naive to understand the problem. When it comes to human problems and human feelings, no one's world is more real than another's. You may have information that your partner doesn't, but you can introduce it without an insult.

24. *Crisis.* Threatening disaster and dire consequences if your partner persists in confronting an issue, such as "Look out now; I've got a short fuse"; "You'll upset Mother (or the children)"; and "If you don't like the way I run this outfit, there's the door." A true fair-chair fight is not possible when one partner feels threatened or encouraged to feel that he or she must walk on eggs.

25. *Invasion.* Forcing yourself into your partner's mind. Some partners are very verbal—others are not. If you, the verbal partner, nag the other with "Talk to me; tell me how you feel" (unless this is the actual subject of the fight), you are invading your partner's privacy. If your partner is willing to make changes to ease the problem, he or she doesn't have to "spill guts" about it as well.

26. *Telepathy.* Faulting your partner for not automatically knowing what you need and want, such as "If you don't know, I can't tell you"; "You should have known that would upset me"; or "You know what I mean!"

27. *Sidetracking.* Inserting comments that are acceptable on their own, but that avoid the issue at hand, such as

"You're beautiful when you're angry," or "You think you've got a problem; let me tell you what I'm facing!"

28. *Nice.* Being overly controlled, soft-spoken, and even-tempered as a manipulating tool to divert your partner's demands. This is a way of not becoming involved in the fight, and a passive-aggressive ploy that is very destructive to your partner and relationship because it is both elusive and indirect.

29. *Soft Spot.* Using an argument or referring to an issue that has been previously established to be a taboo or an extremely sensitive subject with your partner. Attacking a soft spot is hitting below the belt. In fair fighting each partner should be allowed to establish what he or she considers to be below the belt.

WHEN A PARTNER COMMITS A FOUL PLOY

You can disarm a foul ploy in a fair-chair fight, but you must keep three things in mind:

1. We learn to use foul ploys—they are not automatic or inherent. They can be unlearned.

2. Foul ploys are a mutual problem. One partner may be a dirty fighter, but often the other partner falls into the ploy instead of confronting and disarming it.

3. Regardless of how unfair they are, foul ploys constitute an effort to solve the problem. When one partner confronts a foul ploy, he or she should be as cooperative as possible at offering other ways to address the problem. For example:

"I feel bad (guilty or angry) when you keep bringing up occasions in the distant past when you've felt angry with me. Wouldn't you be willing to stay with current occasions so that we can change what's happening without loading them up with history?"

All is not lost just because your partner uses a foul ploy. There is a way to handle it and a way not to.

NEUTRALIZING THE FOUL PLOY

To neutralize a ploy, you must first be able to recognize the ploy itself, which is sometimes hard to do when it is tangled up with the issue.

Imagine yourself busily trying to think through the issue, your own counterissues, your partner's point of view, and possible concessions for both of you, when your partner pushes this Trojan horse into the compound of communication. You start treating it as though it's a legitimate part of the issue, and then you realize, if you are perceptive, that the thing is loaded—a foul ploy.

At this point, you should stop everything and confront the ploy itself by saying, "I think I see a foul ploy here. Could we agree that it is unfair and not relevant to the fight and drop it?" Using some variation of those words is confronting the foul ploy. Sometimes the fight must stop until you call the foul ploy and your partner agrees to stop. If you had a referee, he or she could make the call, but you do not, so you must look out for yourself.

Good fair-chair partners are willing to recognize (even reluctantly) their own foul ploys when their partners point them out. Many foul ploys are accidental or habitual, and partners are unaware of what they have done until the ploys are brought to their attention. People often don't know that they are using a device that is destructive rather than constructive.

IGNORING A PLOY

You have one other acceptable option: dismissing the ploy. To dismiss a ploy you either recognize the ploy and choose to ignore it or excuse it without either confronting it or going along with it. But you can do this only if you can truly continue the fight without playing into the ploy. If your partner is sarcastic, for example, you can note this to yourself and continue, without answering or referring to the sarcasm. However, once you have let it go, you really cannot legitimately call attention to it later, or present your partner with a list of dirty fighting ploys at the end of the fight.

Remember that foul ploys are only fouls when you're sitting in the fair chairs, and you should call them only in a fair fight. No one has agreed not to use foul ploys outside the fair chairs. If your partner is using them outside the chairs, you might want to fight about that ploy in the chairs and try to establish that your partner will not continue to use the ploy in normal conversation.

ENCOURAGING THE FOUL PLOY

Falling into a foul ploy is a bad move because it raises the heat level of the argument. If you don't recognize the foul ploy for what it is and confront it or excuse it, you will probably fall right into your partner's trap. Dr. George Bach calls this collusion: your partner has seduced you into fighting dirty, and feels encouraged to continue being unfair. You are aiding, abetting, and busily refuting an illegitimate argument. Instead of dissolving the error, you have compounded it.

CONFRONTING THE UNAWARE PARTNER

Not everyone you fight with knows the difference between foul ploys and fair fighting, but everyone knows what fair play is all about. Without using special vocabulary, you can point out to any partner that the way he or she is fighting is unnecessary and distracting from your main purpose, which is to solve a problem, and you would appreciate it if you both could continue the fight without being unfair.

STAGE 4
ENDING THE FIGHT

ACTION

12. (Compromise) B tells A what he or she is willing to do.

13. (Compromise) A tells B what compromises he or she is willing to make.

14. A and B both feed back their agreement.

15. (Clean up) A and B both check out whether anything is left unsettled, and if there is, they settle it.

16. (Mutual end) A and B agree to end the fight.

COACHING

Often fair-chair fights are resolved in one sitting because most partners want to solve the problem quickly. In a surprising number of fair fights, when partner A asks for change, partner B realizes for the first time that he or she is creating a stimulus for A's bad feelings. B agrees with A's request for a change, as in "I didn't know that bothered you. Of course I'll stop doing that."

At the end of a fair fight, partners usually experience a surge of good feeling as the accordion of feelings opens up. When partners don't express bad feelings, they neglect their good feelings as well, and the accordion is squeezed tight. But when partners air their negative feelings, the accordion expands in both directions and good feelings start to flow.

By the time they have reached this stage, partners in a fair fight are ready to change. Each has taken seriously the honest words of the other. The "I" has become tempered with the needs of the "you" in the service of the "us." Suddenly all three can be rewarded in a single, clear agreement.

MUTUAL CHANGE

Solutions to deeper problems usually come from some change in both partners. It is unrealistic for the initiator of the fight to expect all the change to come from the other partner. The final measure of fairness in fair-chair fighting is the flexibility of both partners. Complete inflexibility is the final foul ploy. An inflexible partner says, in effect, "What I do and how I do it is more important to me than your bad feelings. You'll have to deal with those bad feelings without help from me."

Both partners need to grow, not one partner at the expense of the other. Both must be willing to change which means they must sacrifice and compromise a little.

When one partner is not concerned with the feelings of the other, the relationship is unhealthy for both partners. For example, "You're the one who wanted this relationship. Take me as I am"; or "You're my mother. I never asked to be here"; or "I had to knuckle under to become a supervisor. Now it's your turn."

A boss cannot survive without loyal employees. Loyal employees don't come with the territory. A boss earns loyalty by caring about the employees' needs.

In the case of "forced partners," such as coworkers who are hired to work together, you still have the advantage that both want a smooth road to travel on, and both normally accept the principle of fair play. (See Upgrading Poor Partners, pp. 75–82.)

In family relationships no one is a prisoner of love—if you don't care about your partner's love, you might lose it. But you are not a prisoner either. Your partner must honor your needs, appropriately if not equally. *In love relationships the partner with the least commitment to the relationship is the one with the most power.*

CHANGE-READINESS VS. NONNEGOTIABILITY

In all of us there is a core of personality that becomes our self-image and emerges in our social behavior. We all have qualities and behaviors that we consider nonnegotiable, but they sometimes become the source of our conflict with others. When you think you have hit upon a nonnegotiable point in your behavior or needs, do not become stubbornly inflexible to change on this point.

There are three ways to reduce conflict without compromising your basic nature:

1. *Negotiate the Nonnegotiability.* Nonnegotiable does not mean unmentionable. Discuss openly what you consider to be your unchangeable core. Explain how strong your feelings are on this point, and make the limits and boundaries clear so that negotiation can still take place outside those limits.

2. *Separate Can't from Won't.* Stop saying, "I simply can't do this, or be this way," when you really mean "I won't." You can change just about anything. Nonnegotiable doesn't mean you can't, but that you feel so strongly about the point that you won't change—changing would threaten too much who you feel you are.

3. *Don't Shut the Door.* How you have been in the past and how you are now are not inevitable prescriptions of how you will be in the future. So when you speak of nonnegotiability, add the word "now." For example, "This point is nonnegotiable to me now."

Then, as in every other conflict, weigh your own needs against the needs of your partner. Think in a fresh way, minimizing past programming, about how much you might be willing to soften on this point.

A TYPICAL FAIR-CHAIR ENDING

A: "I want you to stop smoking. I worry about you, and I also don't like smoke."

B: "It's asking too much for me to stop smoking. But I can cut down on it when we're together."

A: "OK, but I'd still rather spend the evening with you than alone. I don't want you to have to sit out on the porch just to smoke."

B: "Suppose I smoke less when we are driving together or watching television; those are the times when you mention it the most."

A: "I'd like that. I'd find it easier to quit complaining about it."

B: "Agreed." (Both partners feed back until the agreement is totally clear.)

THE FINAL FEEDBACK

Be warned that sometimes partners are so pleased with their final agreement and so flushed with the victory and relief of finishing that they leave the chairs without exchanging the final feedback on their agreement and compromises for the future. Each partner must end the fair-chair fight by reviewing the agreement and conditions: "As I see it, you have promised to do 'such and such' under 'so and so' conditions, and I have agreed to stop doing 'this and that.' "

Often the final feedback reveals something you have forgotten to include or some minor distortion or misunderstanding of your agreement. Don't quit too soon!

THAT UNFINISHED FEELING

To end a fair-chair fight properly, both partners should feel satisfied: their feelings have been heard, changes have been made, and the issue is put to rest. There should be no residual bad feelings. If there are, stay in the chairs and deal with them.

Even after a good fight, something may be amiss with one partner. It is necessary to check this out. A partner may say, "Well, that finishes it for me. Is there anything still bothering you about this?" And the other may still be harboring a small resentment: "Well, at one point when were working on this, I got the impression that you thought I had lied to you, and I'd like to clear that up before we finish." And they do.

Once I initiated a fair fight with my office mate about how he was reporting my telephone messages. We finished the fight amicably, but then he said, "Arthur, I get the impression that I was hearing more anger in you than this issue could generate. Is there something else bothering you?" There was. We dealt with the issue, and my respect for him increased measurably from that day on.

THE FINAL TOUCH

I haven't mentioned this final touch in the Action section because it is optional, and depends on the nature of the relationship. I believe a good fair-chair fight should end with physical contact. A handshake is enough, but where hugging is part of the relationship, this is the place for it.

BROKEN AGREEMENTS

Agreements are broken, even the best of them. This is no cause for alarm or for thinking that fair-chair fighting has failed. A broken agreement signals that the agreement you made doesn't work for the partner who broke it, and that you need to make a new agreement. You must go back to the fair chairs—as often as it takes—to find an agreement that both partners can live with.

Remember, too, that these agreements, like any other contracts, can become outdated. New factors develop. An agreement may be harder to keep than you or your partner predicted. Partners can also be lazy or forgetful. People sometimes break their agreements in retaliation for something new their partner is doing. All this needs to come back to the chairs for renegotiation. Do not expect every agreement to be perfect, and do not be disillusioned when one isn't.

A partner who has made an agreement to compromise may ask for a rematch because the deal is too hard to keep and he or she wishes to renegotiate. When you sit down again to improve an agreement, here is the attitude you should take: "OK, what went wrong? How can we fix it? How can we improve this agreement so that it works?"

WHEN ONCE IS NOT ENOUGH

Not all fair-chair fights are resolved in one sitting. Sometimes partners need to process in private their own needs against the needs of their partner, and then come back with a plan of action. (See Time-Outs, p. 48–49.)

Fair-chair fighting is a constant process, not a one-time thing.

A GOOD, SHORT FAIR-CHAIR FIGHT

STAGE 1: THE APPROACH

1. *J:* (Announcement) I've got a beef with you. Will you work with me on it?

2. *A:* What's it about?

3. *J:* (Nature of problem) It's about your not taking out the garbage.

4. *A:* (Appointment) How about doing it after dinner, before eight o'clock?
   J: OK, after I do the dinner dishes.

STAGE 2: THE BEGINNING

5. *J:* (Taking the chairs) We've got a half-hour before evening television. Let's sit down and start.

6. *J:* (The beef and feelings) Here's my problem. Yesterday, you didn't take out the garbage. You keep saying you'll take out the garbage, but you keep forgetting, and then I get impatient and don't want to bug you, so I take it out myself. I feel like a grouch if I complain about it, and yet I'm beginning to feel put upon, and I'm getting resentful.

7.   *A:* (Feedback) Your beef is that I keep forgetting to take out the garbage, and you are resenting being put in a position where you feel either taken advantage of or forced into complaining to me. And yesterday you took the garbage out yourself.

      J: (Release) That's right.

8.   *A:* (Counter) You're right. I have been forgetting, and I don't mean to, but at the time you mention that the garbage bag is full, I'm usually doing something else or relaxing, and then when I get up, I have forgotten it. Yesterday when you asked, we were watching TV.

9.   *J:* (Feedback) You are admitting that you do forget, but you are saying that the reason is that I tell you about it at a time when you're busy, and then later, you forget.

      A: Right.

STAGE 3: NEGOTIATION

10.   *A:* (Discussion) This shouldn't take too long because I want to find a solution for it, too. I know I have promised to get rid of the garbage, and I'm not doing it. Yesterday when I came to do it, you had already taken it out, and then I felt guilty. So what I really hear you wanting is a way to tell me when the garbage is full without nagging, and what I want is to hear about it when I'm available to take it out, so that I don't have to keep it in mind too long.

      J: That sounds good. What can we do to make that happen?

11.   (No need for time-outs.)

STAGE 4: ENDING THE FIGHT

12.   *A:* (Compromise) How about a silent signal of some
       sort, like putting up a small garbage flag in the hallway
       so that I'll see it when I'm on my feet and passing
       through?

13.   *J:* (Compromise) You want me to put up a flag when
       the garbage is ready? OK, let's try it, so long as you'll
       make the flag and find the place to put it.

14.   *A:* (Agreement feedback) I'll make the flag tonight. You
       put it up when the garbage is ready to go out. I'll take
       out the garbage bag within a couple hours, probably
       the next time I go through the hall.
       J: When the flag is up, I can expect the garbage out in
       hours. Right?
       A: Right.

15.   *A:* (Clean up) Does that do it for you? Anything missing?
       J: Don't make an ugly or conspicuous flag.
       A: Right! And for me, give me a couple days to get used
       to the thing; remind me for a day or so if I'm missing the
       flag.

16.   *J:* (Mutual end) OK. I feel better about it. Let's stop.
       A: Sounds good. I'm finished.

THE DIRTY FIGHT

There are two extremes in fighting with intimates: underkill and overkill. In underkill fighting we want to make our points without risking real confrontation, so we roll over, whine, and complain. In overkill we attack, fighting to win at any price. Most of us are good at both of these, but we leap over the middle ground, which is fair fighting. Here are examples of each:

Underkill: You hurt me when you do things like that. You are being very inconsiderate.

Fair Fighting: I'm feeling uncomfortable with something you do. Can I get your help to change it?

Overkill: Now hear this, mister—you're wrong. Shape up!

Let's take a look at the Bickersons at home, engaging in a traditional dirty fight in which every statement is a foul ploy and gives full permission for a foul ploy in return. Foul ploys build up on one another, until nothing but hostility remains. In this fight, the Bickersons are arguing about taking out the garbage. The referee will call out and identify each foul. Unfortunately, we are likely to see ourselves in more than one of these foul ploys.

She: "This kitchen garbage has been a problem for a long time, you know. I've been after you for three years about it, and I remember that back at the old place, five years ago, you never touched the garbage, even when I was out of town."

Ref: ATTIC (Throwing in the past.)

He: "It seems you're always dissatisfied with me lately. It's either the garbage, or I don't buy the right brand of dog food, or I don't pay enough attention to you, or I spend too much time at the office."

Ref: MULTIPLE LISTING (Listing irrelevant gripes.)

She: "This is sounding more and more like our argument about your not turning the lights out when you leave a room. It took you months to admit you were wrong, and I suppose you're up to your same old resistance to the truth."

Ref: DOGHOUSE (Repeated reference to already admitted faults.)

He: "Well, Princess, maybe you'd like me to just stay home, put on a pretty apron, and wait for you to ring the servant's bell."

Ref: SARCASM (Ironic insult.)

She: "There you go, being childish again. Your mother was a perpetual nag, and you've projected that on me so that every time I need something done, you overreact and get your back up."

Ref: PSYCHIATRY (Giving psychological reasons for your partner's behavior.)

He: "What's that supposed to mean?"

Ref: PARANOIA (Accusing your partner of hidden aggression.)

She: "You know exactly what I'm talking about! And if you don't know by now, I can't tell you."

Ref: TELEPATHY (Expecting your partner to read your mind.)

He: "You have no right to feel this way. It doesn't make sense. Nobody gets this upset over such a little thing as taking out the garbage."

Ref: DISALLOWING (Refusing to accept the legitimacy of your partner's feelings.)

She: "Well, maybe you don't realize it, but lots of our friends mention how insensitive you are. Ask your own sister—she knows!"

Ref: THIRD PARTY (Introducing information and/or opinions of others not available at this moment.)

He: "OK, I give up; I'll take the damned garbage out every damned time you ask me to, no matter what else I'm doing at the time. If you don't appreciate all I do around here, fixing things, walking the dog, keeping the garage clean, and running to the store every time we run out of something, just add this to the list. I'll do it to keep peace around here."

Ref: DOUBLE BIND (Placing your partner in the position that any response will be to his or her disadvantage.)

She: "Oh God! I guess you're right. I try to do the right thing, but I always seem to foul it up. Sometimes I wonder why you were ever interested in me to begin with. I'm no good to anyone anymore. I don't know why I even try."

Ref: MEA CULPA (Milking your partner for sympathy by taking all the blame.)

He: "Look, this is getting us nowhere. I'm a very forgetful person and that's the sum of it. I don't mean to be, but I have no control over it. There are some things you are just going to have to accept about me. It's not deliberate; it's just me."

Ref: THAT'S THE WAY I AM (Hiding behind inner forces that overwhelm personal choice.)

She: "You think you've got a problem! I've been trying to tell you for years that I have no head for figures, and yet you insist that I do all the monthly bills and finances."

Ref: SIDETRACKING (Diverting the attack by introducing a separate issue.)

He: "You've got to realize that people have to adjust to each other if they're going to live together. Now just count up all the good things in your life, and you'll feel much better. This isn't an important matter and you're making far too much of it."

Ref: PARENTING (Controlling and talking down to your partner.)

She: "It just doesn't make any sense. Your own brother George is so thoughtful and considerate of Myra. He anticipates her every need instead of having to be reminded constantly to do the right thing. Why can't you be a little more like him?"

Ref: COMPARISON (Comparing your partner to an ideal or a better person.)

He: "Hold on now! That's typical of you midwestern farm people. You believe life is one big husking bee, with everybody ready to rush to everybody else's every little need. I know the type. You've all got the prairie-home mentality."

Ref: CLASSING (Reducing your partner's individuality by lumping her or him with a group or class.)

She: "Listen, if you were any kind of a man, you'd take some responsibility. I thought I married a real man, not a spoiled brat."

Ref: GENDERING (Applying a sexual stereotype.)

He: "If you'll pardon me, you wouldn't know a real man if you saw him in a *Playgirl* centerfold. I spend every day of my life out in the real world, where your kind of whining would lose you every friend you've got. You've lived your whole life in a protected ivory tower: home, school, and marriage."

Ref: REAL WORLD (Accusing your partner of a lesser life experience.)

She: "Well, you're just Mr. Perfect, aren't you? If you don't think I know that you've been going to a sex therapist for six months to learn what you should know naturally, you're crazy, big guy!"

Ref: SOFT SPOT (Derailing your partner by striking at a known sensitive subject.)

He: "Look out, now! You know I have a short fuse when you talk like that! One more nasty crack like that, and I won't be responsible for what happens!"

Ref: CRISIS (Threatening your partner with a blowup.)

She: "You're really merciless, aren't you? You know very well that these prolonged hassles get me so upset I can't sleep, but you persist in goading me until I'm so sick from it I can't think."

Ref: SICK-OUT (Taking refuge in physical ailments.)

He: "Now you've done it. You always do it. You start a fight, and then you throw in everything but the kitchen sink. I sit down here in good faith to settle this, and you pull out all the stops. You always have to make me look like a villain."

Ref: GUILTING (Appearing to make your partner the aggressor and you the victim.)

She: "Well, I give up. You obviously don't want to cooperate, so I'm going to quit trying to negotiate. It's all uphill. See you in the pigsty, Mr. Wonderful!"

Ref: BREAK OFF (Leaving the fight.)

UPGRADING POOR PARTNERS

You can't use fair fighting effectively until you have convinced yourself that your dominant goal is to remove barriers between you and another person. But there is no guarantee that the other person feels the same way. Ideally, if you've reached the full fair-fight stance, you are in a power position made up of three factors:

1. You care about the feelings of the other.

2. You are ready to treat the other fairly. You have now adopted this assumption: I am important; my needs are important. You are important; your needs are important.

3. You are aware of the difference between clean and dirty fighting and you understand the rules of fair fighting.

But a boss, an associate, or an intimate may not be caring, fair, or aware, and whatever he or she is missing, you must make up for in the fair fighting yourself.

You have one of several attitude combinations to confront in any partner who has not read this book. In the following diagram I have listed the attitude combinations in order of increasing difficulty. Below each combination is your appropriate response.

	Ideal	Cooperative	Approachable	Defended
Your Partner	Caring Fair Aware	Caring Fair Unaware	Uncaring Fair Unaware	Uncaring Unfair Unaware
Your Response	Confront as needed	Request familiarity with fair-fighting process	Persistent Consistent Unilateral fairness	Persistent Consistent Soft response, Unilateral fairness

IMPROVING YOUR PARTNER

1. The Ideal Partner. With an ideal partner you have a safe, trusting, and skillful relationship in which both partners know the fair-chair fight process.

Ideal

Caring
Fair
Aware

Goal: Quick, painless resolution of your problem.

Who is this? Your intimate-other, or a close, trusted partner.

Response: Confront each other openly as needed.

2. The Cooperative Partner

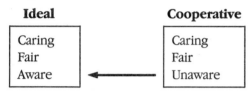

Ideal   **Cooperative**

Ideal	Cooperative
Caring	Caring
Fair	Fair
Aware ←	Unaware

Goal: To change an unaware partner into an aware one.

Who is this? An open intimate-other, or a close partner.

Response: Request him or her to become familiar with the fair- chair process.

This partner has all the fair fighting qualities except for awareness of how to fair fight. Ask your partner to learn the process with you, read the manual, and practice on small issues. You can help change this person from being an unaware to an aware partner.

3. The Approachable Partner

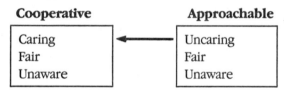

Cooperative   **Approachable**

Cooperative	Approachable
Caring ←	Uncaring
Fair	Fair
Unaware	Unaware

Goal: To move a fair partner toward being a caring one.

Who is this? An egocentric intimate-other, or an aloof associate.

Response: Persistent, consistent, unilateral fairness.

This partner is the typical reasonable boss, colleague, roommate, or friend. This could also describe an egocentric but reasonable family member. Uncaring usually means that this partner feels no particular need to care about your emotional stance and doesn't expect you to care in return.

This partner believes that so long as the two of you honor the rules and commitments of your relationship, caring about feelings is an unnecessary distraction and he or she will avoid serious encounters with negative feelings. But he or she also has a fair and honorable self-image and would not deliberately cause pain to a partner. Since this partner is unaware of fair-fight procedures and would probably think them unnecessary, his or her self-image of fairness is your only reasonable entry point.

So you now have a situation that requires, above all, that you consistently apply fairness, following the rules of fair fighting alone and teaching them to your partner only through your own example. You need to be caring, fair, and aware, but require only fairness in return. In every encounter address the issue in terms of fairness. Remind your partner in as many authentic and varied ways as you can that you see him or her as a fair person, especially in your relationship.

This is where persistence comes in. So long as you continue to have negative feelings, and therefore a problem, you need to confront this partner with consistent fairness as often as your relationship can take it. Don't become a pest, but return persistently to your partner to address your problem.

But don't rely only on repetition: Simply repeating your position will encourage your partner to be less fair rather than more. Your ultimate goal is to help this partner add caring to fairness, not push him or her toward exasperation and eventual entrenchment. As new feelings and new insights appear to you, return to this person and voice them, always with consistent fairness.

4.   The Defended Partner

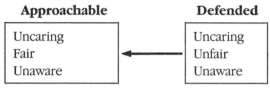

Approachable   **Defended**

Uncaring	Uncaring
Fair	Unfair
Unaware	Unaware

Goal: To move your partner from the unfair to the fair position.

Who is this? An immature intimate-other, or an insensitive or hostile associate.

Response: Persistent, consistent, soft response, unilateral fairness.

These partners are so extremely defensive and self-protective that they cannot afford to be either caring or fair. The key to these people is defensiveness. If you can reduce that and encourage them to believe in your own good faith (not necessarily friendship), they will feel that it's safe to relax the defenses and be fair.

As a fair fighter, this is your greatest test. You must now keep four balls in the air: persistence, consistency, soft response, and unilateral fairness.

Persistence will be much harder with this partner. Until you can change unfairness to fairness, every encounter can be painful. You will have to endure insults, sarcasm, intimidation, and direct hostility. You will want to quit trying. The relationship itself will have to be important enough for you to keep going.

This person may be your boss, a competitive colleague, a customer, a supplier, even your own child, sibling, parent, or intimate-other. You may care about this person or you may not, but in either case your motivation to improve the situation must be strong.

Using the consistency of fair fighting is vital. Each time you play into a foul ploy, or counterattack, you add to his or her belief that you are an opponent, not a trustworthy partner, and he or she will be delighted to have flushed out your antagonism, proving that defensiveness toward you is necessary and useful.

You must carry every aspect of fair fighting alone, stating the problem as your own, feeding back responses to his or her satisfaction, sidestepping foul ploys, and trying constantly to see your partner's point of view while pressing your own.

Because of his or her defensiveness, this partner will usually avoid all occasions where you can sit alone together and talk seriously. You may need to use every possible kind of contact just to be heard—making your points on the fly, in the car, when others are present, over the phone, or even by notes, memos, or correspondence.

Your final tool in this long-term strategy is to employ the soft response, a technique found in the martial arts. The idea is to absorb the counterattack. This takes inner determination, some skill, and a firm sense of personal self-worth. It is an exercise in inner strength and self-choice. You try to be positive toward your partner while avoiding his or her attacks. You absorb or pass through the attacks without letting them distract your own purpose. The goal in soft martial arts is to allow your opponents to do anything they want without their hurting you. We use three basic tactics: adhering, yielding, and discharging.

An opponent in physical fighting expects to have space to swing a punch and a solid target to stop its forward motion. We deprive our opponent of both. Instead, we physically join with him or her, hand against fist, so the strike becomes nothing more than a push. Then, if we yield and move backward as the strike occurs, adhering, or staying with it, all the while, there is no solid target, and the opponent goes beyond his or her own point of balance. Then, by turning aside, we discharge, or allow the opponent to pass through, because he or she has lost balance and overextended the energy of the strike.

In a verbal fight we adhere by feeding back the argument; we yield by recognizing the partner's feelings and absorbing any insult, sarcasm, or accusation; and we discharge by not responding to the thrust, but letting it pass through, unbalanced and unengaged. The fair fighter slows down the pace and allows self-control to operate full time by choosing the most productive rather than the most instinctive response.

THE UNEXPECTED BONUS

In many cases, you'll find a strange but gratifying change occurring. In order to avoid your determined, persistent attempts to confront, your partner may begin to change his or her behavior and start compromising, but never admitting to it, just to get away from your persistent, consistent pressure. You may even get exactly what you have been asking for, but without your partner making any open concessions.

THEORY OF THE SQUEAKY WHEEL

In the physical, chemical, and social sciences the principle of the squeaky wheel holds true: a persistent irritant within an organism will ultimately change the nature of the entire organism in the direction of its influence. To be persistent, however, the irritant must avoid being forced out in the process.

In fair fighting, the organism is your relationship with a partner. By persisting without attacking, you hold the relationship together long enough for your effects (the meeting of your needs) to work.

Look at the diagram again. In the worst of all worlds, you have a partner who is uncaring, unfair, and unaware. By persistent fair fighting, you can change unfairness to fairness, noncaring to caring, and finally, unawareness to awareness. Any one of these changes is a dramatic improvement in the relationship and a reduction of the problem.

	Ideal	**Cooperative**	**Approachable**	**Defended**
Your Partner	Caring Fair Aware ← Unaware	Caring ← Uncaring Fair Unaware	Uncaring Fair ← Unfair Unaware	Uncaring Unfair Unaware
Your Response	Confront as needed	Request familiarity with fair-fighting process	Persistent Consistent Unilateral fairness	Persistent Consistent Soft response, Unilateral fairness

BLACK BELT FIGHTING

To change from being dirty fighters to being clean, fair-chair fighters, we have to start at the beginning and learn to fight all over again, this time to win together with our partners, not over them. This first level of fair-chair fighting is white belt fighting: it is a simple process that provides partners with experience, and gives them confidence in themselves, their relationship, and the fair fighting process.

THE BLACK BELT OPTION

When the time comes that both partners feel really secure with the process, they may try some black belt encounters. Black belt fighting is more complex and, for a beginner, more troubling. You have to know the rules and how to apply them in order to enter the lists of advanced fair-chair fighters. When you feel ready for this, try the techniques below.

HAIRCUT* AND BACKCUT

Beginning fighters, the white belt partners, consider blowing up a major foul ploy as in the ploys Land Mine and Crossfire.

*Haircut originated in the Synanon Games in the 1960s.

But skilled black belt fighters can handle a controlled blowup so long as they follow special rules. Blowups are the forest fires of fair fighting. Painful as they are, blowups can be controlled if you know how.

Suppose that partner A is suddenly generating a lot of anger at partner B and is ready to blow. If the feelings are honest, there must be a way for A to dump this load on B, and make it clear that he or she is too angry for normal fair fighting. The technique to use is a carefully controlled emotional blast called a haircut.

Haircut.   The furious partner A comes to partner B and says, "I've got a lot to say to you, and I want to give you a haircut" (or some similar words). B gets ready and gives the go-ahead. A rages for a specified time limit of two minutes. Partners can decide on their own time limit, but it should be under five minutes, and they must keep to the limit. This is the only place in fair-chair fighting where we allow foul ploys without challenge.

Partner B, no matter how devastated or angry at this blast, cannot respond to the haircut, but just sits silently and takes it. As a black belt fighter, B patiently waits for his or her turn. All B can say when it is over is, "OK, I hear you."

The partners take an immediate half-hour break. They get away from each other during that time. Partners may decide on a longer time-out if they wish.

Backcut.   When the half-hour is up, partner A must be ready and available for a backcut. A must be willing to receive the backcut—under the same restrictions that partner B had to endure. Now it's B's turn to tell A anything he or she wants for exactly two minutes. A can only respond at the end with, "OK, I hear you."

One more rule. Never, never may partner A or partner B hold each other responsible for, or refer again to, what he or she has heard in the haircut or backcut outside of the fair chairs. Whatever they say at that time dies within those two-minute time periods.

If, however, either partner wishes to bring up any issue from a haircut or backcut, he or she may raise it as a gripe in a fair fight, but not outside the chairs. In that fair fight, the partners must hold to all of the rules of fair-chair fighting, especially the taboo on foul ploys. Foul ploys are free throws in haircut and backcut—they are forbidden in fair-chair fighting.

White belt fighters cannot easily handle such high emotions. Only after much fair-chair practice can they conduct a clean fight based on an explosion like a haircut or backcut. Use these two escape valves rarely.

GROUPING

In white belt fighting, only single, current, and specific issues are acceptable in the fair chairs. A partner may not expand the fight beyond one recent incident. Black belt fighters are ready to take on larger gripes that are correctable even though they cover multiple incidents over a period of time. In grouping, partner A may put several related incidents together in a single fight.

A: I feel as though you've been taking me for granted lately, and that's the issue I want to talk about, but I can't make the point with a single incident only, so I'm going to mention the last three times I've felt this way. I want to group these incidents.

Partners A and B now have two ways to go. They will either agree to take each incident and handle it, or decide to go straight to the overall issue of whether B is taking A for granted and what they can do about it.

HISTORY

I consider history to be a foul ploy in white belt fighting because we usually can't correct incidents from the past. There is little or no opportunity for changing something that is already closed and covered over by more recent problems. But black belt partners may wish to clear up some of their previous bad feelings. Even though the issue can't be corrected, one partner has been holding on to bad feelings about it and needs to tell the other about them. Think of a history fight as an information session or clearinghouse for old feelings.

> *A:* I want to do a history with you. I'm not asking for a change, but maybe you can tell me something that will help me feel less bothered about this. Last summer I heard you telling a new employee that he was hired to get things up to speed around here, and I felt that you were criticizing my speed. I've been feeling resentful ever since.

VAGUE ISSUE

You place a partner at an unfair advantage when you cannot be specific about your beef. For this reason, bringing up a vague issue is dirty fighting. But there are times when a person has a bad feeling about a partner for which he or she has no particulars. As a black belt fighter who has had plenty of experience fighting about specific problems, you can now ask for a confrontation on a vague feeling. For example:

> *A:* "I need to air a vague gripe with you because I can't find any particular incidents to support it. You've seemed very withdrawn around me lately. I can't put my finger on it, but I have started to feel uncomfortable about it. I don't know

where I am with you. Don't ask me when or where I've picked this up because I can't answer that. But that's my problem."

SHARED FIGHTING

Except for fighting in front of trainers, referees, or counselors, white belt people should fight alone. But black belt fighters find it useful to fight in front of others. Remember that by the time you are a black belt fair-chair fighter, fights are very open and constructive.

Good fighters fight best when others are present. Perhaps they are just showing off, or maybe they are afraid to present an image of being unfair. For whatever reason, fights are lighter, more humorous, fairer, and more flexible when done in front of other adults.

Fair fighting between two people can be appropriate in a staff meeting without embarrassment. At home at the dinner table, a father-mother fair fight is good for the children. It reduces rather than increases the children's anxiety over their parents' relationship.

But don't go public until you're ready, otherwise you might feel as if you are performing and that you must win in order to look good.

Remember, if you are fighting too much, on either the white or black belt level, you may need the help of a professional.

THE WHITE/BLACK TRANSITION

There is no graduation ceremony from white belt to black belt fighting. The time to cross the line is when both partners have used fair-chair fighting long enough and often enough to trust each other and the fair-chair fight process. Remember: Do not use black belt processes on white belt fighters. That is not fair fighting.

THE ANATOMY OF ANGER

Anger is natural and inevitable, but unlike quiet emotions like grief or tenderness, anger is so volatile that two myths have grown up around it: First, that anger is triggered automatically, causing people to become victims of their own anger; second, that anger needs expression, and therefore the healthiest way to experience anger is to let it out rather than to hold it in.

Do we control anger, then, or don't we? Is it good or bad to let anger out in a social situation?

WHO CONTROLS YOUR ANGER?

Stop saying that you can't control your anger. You do control it. And, if you look inside yourself, you will realize that you also choose to be angry. We would like to believe that anger can run away with us because then we are not responsible for the anger. This is not true. We release our anger as surely as a handler slips the collar from an attack dog and gives the signal to lunge.

But anger is hard to admit to. An "uncontrollable" anger against others gives us our license to perform a wide range of anti-social behavior without penalty. Anger is even the loophole of the law courts—committing a crime in righteous anger gains sympathy from the court and traditionally lessens the severity of the sentence. Anger is considered a mitigating circumstance, and we cherish and preserve this little lifetime insurance policy.

Controlling anger and choosing anger, however, are not the same. When we control our anger, we let it happen internally, but we also place an energy against it to hold it in and prevent it from showing. When we choose our anger, on the other hand, we go deeper, to the source of the anger. Choosing anger is the process of deciding whether or not you will allow yourself to feel angry, or choose another reaction instead.

Both choosing and controlling anger have two psychological sources within us, and it is the confusion of those sources that creates the myth about uncontrollable anger.

CATEGORY IS THE FIRST SOURCE

Anger may have been useful to you in the past, since it is often reinforced by the behavior of others. People pay attention when you are angry. They give way a little or a lot. For a few brief moments, you are the priority that they must deal with. So anger can be rewarding, especially considering that much anger originates in the feeling that you are not being taken as seriously or as importantly as your own self-image requires.

Your memories are filed away in categories that tell you how you respond in certain situations. Let's take an instance. You have been insulted before in your lifetime, and you were, for that moment, angry about it. You file this incident in your "I've been insulted" category in your mental computer with all your other memories. The next time you are insulted, your mental computer calls up this category, and on the screen flashes the whole file, along with your past emotional response: anger. In a situation where rapid action also seems appropriate, the angry feeling quickly becomes an angry outburst.

In a category-triggered response like the one I just described, anger has seemed automatic. But you have the choice to put your automatic anger through a second process to cool it before you explode.

MULTISELF IS THE REAL CHOOSER

Most of us do not take into consideration that there is a second process that follows the automatic anger trigger. For any triggered emotion to become an acceptable response, it must pass through the multiself, and the multiself has the final say in deciding whether you will choose to go with the triggered emotion or send down to your computer for another, different response.

In a normal person, the second process (multiself) always has priority and power over the first (category). The two processes act very much like a computer and its user. The computer (category) shows what it has stored, and the user (multiself) decides whether that's the action to take or not.

There's one more complication. Each of us is a multiself. The multiself is made up of several subselves, and although they may often act in unison, the subselves often conflict with one another. To help us understand how the multiself works, many psychologists describe it as containing a Child subself, a Parent subself, and an Adult subself.

The subselves act according to their roles, and generally follow a predictable pattern. For example, the Child, when insulted, might choose to be angry. The Parent subself might insist that an angry outburst is too antisocial. The Adult might

LETS HAVE IT OUT

swing its weight to either choice, depending on what response seems most appropriate to the situation.

WHAT MADE ME DO THAT?

When we are suddenly angry and then later regret it, we say things like "My anger ran away with me," or "I wasn't myself," or "I don't know what made me say that." All these statements come from the multiself trying to shirk responsibility for having let an "automatic" emotion pass through to the behavior level without processing it thoroughly.

The truth is that the multiself is always there and always in power, but because of internal wrangling among the subselves, one subself may quickly grab power and push the automatic emotion through to action without proper consultation with the other subselves.

That's why it often seems as though the multiself abdicates its power over choices. Not choosing is in itself a choice that we often find convenient to ignore or deny.

THE SEVEN-SECOND LIMITATION

Recent anger studies have measured the duration of an angry emotion. It doesn't last for weeks or days or even minutes—it lasts seven seconds. To last longer, anger must be rekindled or nourished.

Let's reconstruct how anger works inside of you at the time of an insult.

1.   Anger appears suddenly on the mental screen that is programmed by your categories.

2. A single subself such as the Child rushes the angry emotion through, without full processing by your other subselves.

3. The preprogrammed anger becomes your behavior of the moment (the seven-second phenomenon).

4. Then, the committee of subselves meet to consider the action. If the Child remains dominant, the anger is rekindled. If not, the emotion dies away, like the sound of a shot fired prematurely.

Your mother was correct in telling you to count to ten before letting your anger take over. To delay is to freeze anger at the flash point and bring in the better judgment of your committee of subselves.

Hatred can last, resentment can endure, dissatisfaction and frustration can be lifetime companions, but a simple instance of true anger lasts only seven seconds unless reinforced.

Recent research leads to the conclusion that acting out your anger tends to fan and rekindle it, and does not, as we have been thinking for years, reduce the pressure and make it go away.

ANGER AS THE WARRIOR EMOTION

But when current researchers try to isolate anger from other emotions, they are surprised to find that anger is usually entwined with other negative emotions and may even be merely a response to them. You may be feeling anxious, depressed, disappointed, frustrated, hurt, or threatened. These are somewhat passive emotions. Anger becomes the active champion of these emotions, ready to do battle to relieve them.

In fair-chair fighting, when you clear away the anger, you often reveal the negative feelings that anger is championing, and you can report these deeper feelings more accurately.

In realizing that anger has two sources, the filed response and the multiself choice, we lose a myth and gain a power. The myth we lose is that other people cause our anger, whereas in truth they only stimulate it. We choose to respond with anger.

Our power is the knowledge that anger is not the wild horse within us that we have been fearing to let out. We can choose not to be angry, and that choice results in power, control, and self- direction. If others cannot make me angry, I am in a powerful position.

DOWNSHIFTING ANGER

Only you can say when and where you need to be angry, and you do make that choice. What we have been calling automatic anger is just quick anger. It is the anger that Horace described as "a brief madness," a sudden, quenchable spark of common insanity. Quick anger is socially allowable in short spurts because it is such a common reaction. But to carry it beyond its own limited flash is to use your own irrationality as a tool to demand change in others.

Once you go beyond the seven-second limit of quick anger, you are clearly choosing to be angry. To ensure that your decision is the wisest one available, you need to try reevaluating your other categories to see if any of them would work just as well. I call this downshifting, a deliberate reasoning process that involves some delay or pause, just like downshifting the gears in your car.

When downshifting, you conduct an inner dialogue among your subselves to come to a new decision or choice regarding your anger. You might eventually decide that you do, in fact, choose to be angry, but a delay always puts the more considered choice on top.

THE DELAY COMMAND

In order to downshift, you must build another category into your categorical system. This new category triggers as fast as any anger category and contains the instant command to delay. The delay command gives you time to downshift and mobilize your total multiself to take over.

The multiself modifies, denies, or approves the anger. After this processing, you may still choose to be angry, but in this case it is fully backed by the subselves, and you are willing to take full responsibility for it.

ANGER AS SELF-INJURY

Once you are aware that you choose to feel angry, you must also know that you choose when and where to express it. Now we come to the second set of major questions about anger: Does it help us internally to let it out? To what degree is anger useful in our encounters with others?

ANGER AS INNER POISON

For years we have been operating on the theory that it is bad for us to hold anger in, in the belief that to contain our anger is to create stress that causes dangerous and painful body symptoms. We know that anger releases adrenaline, the hormone that prepares us for fight or flight, and that when we do not use up this energy for those purposes, but hold it in, it bounces around the system and does damage. We suffer from mental distraction, headaches, numerous digestive disorders (from indigestion and ulcers to constipation), high blood pressure, insomnia, and more. Catharsis has been thought to vent the anger and let it go, much as releasing a bull into the rodeo ring stops him from chewing up the chute.

Recent studies, however, support a new theory that the stress that anger creates need not be damaging. We know that holding in anger is dangerous because it creates stress, but there is both unhealthy and healthy stress—therefore damaging and undamaging anger. Many people thrive on certain kinds of stress, and their secret appears to be that stress is acceptable when it is their way of controlling or easing negative situations.

Consider the research findings below that show how stress may be reduced in anger, and note how fair-chair fighting responds to these conditions.

RESEARCH FINDINGS

Suppressed anger is unlikely to have medical consequences

- If we feel in control of the situation that is causing the anger

- If we interpret the anger as a sign of a grievance to be corrected instead of an emotion to be sullenly protected

- If we feel committed to the work and people in our lives[1]

---

1. Carol Tavris, *Anger: The Misunderstood Emotion* (New York: Touchstone, Simon & Schuster, Inc., 1982), p. 119.

FAIR-CHAIR RESPONSE

- Although others can stimulate our anger, each of us is the cause and controller of his or her own anger.

- We use anger to correct a grievance and do not allow it to turn to sullenness.

- Fair-chair fighting helps us be committed to the work and people in our lives because it is our active move toward resolution and intimacy.

So anger (and its underlying stress) can be healthy if we use it positively, but unhealthy if we view it as a symptom of helplessness and separation.

But by far the most persuasive argument of new research is that where we once acted on the theory that aggression helped us to get in touch with our feelings, we now consider that aggression frequently has the opposite effect of inflaming the anger, not reducing it.

LETTING OUT ANGER

Venting rage can make you angrier, not less angry. When children are angry, research shows that their anger is not reduced by talking about it (for talking anger out seems more to rehearse than reduce it), nor playing with guns and other aggressive toys, but by being helped to understand why the person who made them angry did so. This last solution, of course, is one of the principal objectives of fair fighting—asking your partner to explain his or her position.

Catharsis is useful, but purely venting emotion is not. In marriage, partners who yell at each other increase rather than decrease their anger. The anger can remain or even get worse if the partners don't find some resolution, but "unfortunately, most people don't know how to express anger without attacking or belittling." [2]

Eliminating foul ploys in fair fighting allows confrontation without attacking and belittling.

USING ANGER AS A TOOL

I remember when the anthropologist Richard Leakey was working in the Olduvai Gorge and updating us regularly on how many thousands of years ago humans began using tools. One colleague of Leakey's was amused at the use of the word "tool." "Those antelope thighbones were no tools," he said. "They were weapons!" Our analogous question is, "When does the tool of anger become a weapon?"

Having established that anger is a chosen emotion, not an automatic one, and that it is not always physically therapeutic to let it out, we should consider how practical is its effect in human relations.

EFFECT OF ANGER ON OTHERS

It may be therapeutic to let our anger out, to fall on punching bags, blocks of wood, or jogging paths, but its effect when directed at others is almost always a negative one. It creates rather than solves problems.

The issue seems to lie not so much in whether or not we use anger, but how we use it. To use anger as a threat to others makes you appear as a foolish, unreliable, and self-centered child. The anger we show may make an effective battle flag

---

2. Tavris, p. 129.

with which to enter the arena, but when we use it as a spear, we tend to trip over it. Aristotle gave neither anger nor hatred any positive use, saying, "Anger is hot and seeks to injure; hatred is cold and seeks to destroy."

Injury, retaliation, and withdrawal appear to be the chief effects of using anger as a weapon. These are the costs of putting fireworks into your front line. Righteous anger, the rage of the warrior, is best used on enemies, not friends or partners. It is heavy weaponry, a total rather than a measured response.

When deciding to release your anger at someone, you must consider the effects on, and the possible countermeasures of, those whom you have shot full of your anger. An eight-hundred-pound gorilla may sleep anywhere he pleases, but the territory is all he gets. He gets no love, no help, no understanding.

A TOOL VS. A WEAPON

In fair-chair fighting, we do not point our anger at each other, we point to our anger—as a symptom that something is wrong that needs correcting. To aim the anger directly at our partner causes the anger itself to become the problem, and the partner then addresses the anger rather than removing whatever triggered it.

I can say, "I am angry with you. Let's do something about it," rather than throwing my anger at you so that its full force will leave me and infect you. Anger is not a constructive negotiating device. We can use it to cause fear, guilt, or even sympathy, but these are foul ploys, not constructive acts of negotiation.

Many psychologists therefore distinguish verbal aggression ("You bitch," or "I'll kill you!") from reporting one's anger ("I'm hopping mad"). . . . Verbal aggression usually fails because it riles up the other person and makes him or her inclined to strike back, whereas a description of your state of mind constitutes less of an attack, inspiring the other person to make amends.[3]

Anger may release the chemistry of courage and give us the impulse to act, but we do little else than create more problems when we use the fuel as the tool. Anger, like pain, means that there is something wrong with your life. When in physical pain, we tell the doctor about it, we do not make him feel it also by screaming or stomping on his foot. Anger, like pain, is a symptom that needs to be reported.

OVERUSE OF ANGER

Discussing our anger can lead to practical solutions, but it can also become obsessive and tiresome. Constant complaining, nagging, bickering, and confronting, no matter how constructively produced, can place too much burden on our partners and can cause them to withdraw rather than be intimate and understanding.

Psychologist Walter Kieckel sums up the difference between the tool and the weapon of anger: "What's called for today is not the ungoverned gush of raw feelings but a new civility that accommodates the expression of angry emotions."[4]

---

3. Tavris, p. 129.
4. Tavris, p. 119.

And Carol Tavris, one of our most authoritative psychologists on anger, sums up the whole purpose of fair fighting with the most useful of approaches: "Good manners melt resentment because they maintain respect between the disagreeing partners."[5]

To me, this translates: "Tell me about your anger, but don't use it on me."

BEST ATTITUDE, BEST RESPONSE

So we come down to two major responses to anger:

1. Know that you can rechoose your emotion. You can reduce your anger internally by delaying response and downshifting to subself negotiation.

2. Don't point your anger at your partner: it can hurt, frighten, or stimulate retaliation. Your anger also advertises a determination to win. Tell your partner about your anger, without acting it out. Use your anger as fuel, not tool.

---

5. Tavris, p. 64.

WHAT TO DO WHEN SOMEONE COMES AT YOU ANGRY

It may be your own partner who comes at you in anger, but it is as likely to be a coworker, a customer, a neighbor, or a total stranger.

Unless you really want the kind of fight we hope to avoid in fair-chair fighting (and there may be times when all you may want is a verbal brawl), then you must switch immediately into a controlled response the moment an angry person approaches you. (We are not discussing a full Land Mine here, merely an angry attack. When faced with fury, back off entirely.)

The first rule with an angry person is that you don't ever react automatically, which means either defensively or offensively. You must make an almost opposite choice. You must recognize and, through feedback, verbalize their anger.

Keep in mind that when an angry person comes at you, he or she wants to do two things: to let you know how angry he or she is and to give you a problem.

When you react defensively, you have accepted the problem. When you react offensively, you are trying to give that person still another problem—your own anger.

But when you hold off your own response and instead listen and feed back, you accomplish wonderful things:

1. You hold the problem where it is—with the angry person—until you're ready to accept it.

2. You defuse the high level of anger by assuring the angry person that you hear him or her. You accept the feelings, but a fight has not yet begun because you are not fighting. There is still time for a cooler encounter.

Most angry people welcome the opportunity to back off from anger once they know it has been heard and accepted.

Use the skills of the soft martial arts, letting your opponents do anything they want so long as they don't hurt you: (1) adhere, (2) absorb, and (3) discharge.

To adhere, get close to your angry opponent by listening to the anger and restating it in feedback. (This is the move an opponent least expects.) Remember that if you are close to your opponent, he or she cannot strike you, for you are too close to the source of the strike.

Absorbing your opponent's energy is easy now. He or she expects you to strike out (offensively) or retreat (defensively). But you do neither; instead, you process his or her anger, and your opponent is left with no offensive thrust to parry and no defensive target for the anger energy.

The force of the attack lessens as you listen and feed back without accepting the problem as your own.

Mother: You're just a no-good, ungrateful brat!

Daughter: You're furious at me and believe I'm worthless and ungrateful.

In combat, you would then discharge your opponent, letting the bull through the cape. But in communication, we usually want resolution of some sort, so rather than discharging the energy of a charging opponent, we want to convert it into fair—or at least civilized—fighting toward resolution.

You do this by moving firmly, but without the flash of anger, from the "you" statements of feedback to the "I" statements of response.

I feel like I don't deserve all the resentment you are giving me.

not

You have no right to talk to me like that.

This is the way to avoid unnecessary fights.

Feelings

No, I'm not just feeling angry, I'm feeling:

agitated

antagonistic

bitchy

bitter

cross

defensive

disagreeable

disgusted

displeased

frustrated

fuming

furious

grouchy

grumpy

hostile

incensed

indignant

irked

irritated

jealous

mad

miffed

outraged

peeved

provoked

resentful

riled

No, I'm not just feeling put down, I'm feeling:

belittled

mortified

embarrassed

picked on

exploited

plagued

harassed

unimportant

humiliated

victimized

insulted

No, I'm not just feeling confused, I'm feeling:

amazed

astonished

baffled

confounded

dazed

disoriented

flabbergasted

flustered

helpless

lost

mixed up

mystified

paralyzed

perplexed

puzzled

rattled

shocked

stumped

surprised

trapped

uncertain

No, I'm not just feeling moody, I'm feeling:

bored

critical

doubtful

drained

impatient

restless

tired

uninterested

No, I'm not just feeling afraid, I'm feeling:

apprehensive

alarmed

anxious

bothered

concerned

fearful

frantic

frightened

horrified

nervous

terrified

uncertain

uneasy

uptight

worried

No, I'm not just feeling dejected, I'm feeling:

beaten down
defeated
depressed
desolate
desperate
devastated
disappointed
discouraged
dismayed
distressed
disturbed
downhearted
forlorn

gloomy
guilty
hopeless
inferior
lonely
miserable
moody
overburdened
overwhelmed
pained
pessimistic
sad
unfulfilled

No, I'm not just feeling rejected, I'm feeling:

abandoned
abused
beaten
betrayed
blocked
bugged
cheated
crushed
cut off
deceived
defenseless
disgraced

friendless
heartbroken
hurt
intimidated
left out
manipulated
mistreated
neglected
offended
snubbed
unappreciated

IF THIS IS FAIR-CHAIR FIGHTING, WHERE ARE WE NOW?

AN OUTLINE OF THE FAIR FIGHT

Prefight Preparation

Who has the problem? You do, if you have the negative feelings. Are you ready? Not if you're aiming to hurt, win, be right, produce guilt, or dump.

Stage 1: The Approach

1. (Announcement) A says, "I've got a problem, gripe, beef, peeve, a bone to pick with you."

2. B says, "OK, what's it about?"

3. A tells B the nature of the problem, but no details.

4. A and B make an appointment to hash it out.

Stage 2: The Beginning

5. You're now sitting in two facing chairs, with no distractions and having scheduled at least a half-hour free time.

6. A says, "Here's my problem, and here's how it makes me feel about you."

7. B feeds back that entire message without adding anything until A agrees that B has heard correctly.

8.   B then counters by giving whatever response he or she thinks is appropriate.

9.   A feeds back that entire message to B's satisfaction.

Stage 3: Negotiation

10.   A and B negotiate, feeding back to each other at all crucial points (no required structure).

11.   A and B stay locked in, keeping the following attitudes up front:
      a. Maintain good faith
      b. Stay authentic, realistic, involved, and good natured
      c. Stay focused on the issue
      d. Introduce and negotiate their demands of each other
      e. Avoid foul ploys, or confront them when they appear
      f. If either A or B recognizes an emotional overload, or an undeniable distraction arises, both agree to a short time-out and reschedule their encounter

Stage 4: Ending the Fight

12.   (Compromise) B tells A what he or she is willing to do.

13.   (Compromise) A tells B what compromises he or she is willing to make as well.

14.   A and B both feed back their agreement.

15.   (Clean up) A and B both check out whether anything is left unsettled, and if there is, they settle it.

16.   (Mutual end) A and B agree to end the confrontation.

About the Author

Dr. Arthur S. Hough, Jr., is professor of communication at San Francisco State University and also has taught in this field at six other American universities. After having completed a B.S. in English Education at Rutgers University, he earned an M.A. and a Ph.D. in Communication Theory from Northwestern University and the University of Denver. He has received one national and three university awards for meritorious teaching.

Dr. Hough was a communication workshop leader at Esalen Institute and other growth centers in the 1960s and has since taught communication and counseling workshops for a dozen government agencies and independent organizations.

Among his publications are three other communication texts: *The Forgotten Choice: Breaking Through Paradigm to Human Potential, Pulling Yourself Together: The Bare-Bones Manual of Subself Negotiation, and Dynamic Silence: A First Book in Concentrative Meditation.*

Note from the Author

Have you any feedback for me that will help make this book more useful and understandable to someone like you (or your partner)?

If you have, please address it to:

Dr. Arthur Hough, Professor of Communication,
BCA Department, San Francisco State University,
1600 Holloway Avenue, San Francisco, CA 94132

#45 -- how do I share w/ others that I'm hurting?
  - read this one again --

#47 -- Keep a journal of thoughts & feelings.
#48 -- Amen!! Think Prayer will work? Let's try it!
#49 -- Poem -
#50 -- Why am I doing this -- hold out hope -- is it
  for me -- am I being selfish.

#52 Learn how to do this - believe.
#53 -- I need to -
#54 - great poem except for the one sentence -
#55 -- how much time is needed?
#56 -- Try this!
#57 -- and this one to -- use Wings topes
#58 -- I used to know how to do this
#60 -- is this where carol is? (poem)
#61 --   "   "   " ?
#65 -- good poem - also -- we're not perfect
#67 -- I probably haven't learned some
#69 --- Am I willing move to that
#70 --- new stereo equip.
#71 -- Good Advise --
#72 -- does fly tying &

10/8/78

How to Survive —

#1 -- I Know t!

#3 -- Im not there yet--

#5 -- How do you feel learn how to "feel."?

#7 -- poem -

#9 -- poem -

#11 -- good exercise --use it!!

#12 -- my sleep habits have changed.-- *no problem falling asleep -- wake at 2-3 cant get back to sleep.*

#14 -- its ok to put some things off.

#15 -- this good because live sure been doing it.

#18 -- my circle of friends is soo small.

#19 -- try this!!

#24 -- Im not looking forward to the Holidays --alone-

#25 -- How can you mourn when you havent given up hope

#27 -- do something about linda S. --Now -

#28 -- Is this whats driving Carol? We need to talk this thru & make sure this is what we want to do.

#29 -- ?

#36 -- let it out --

#37 -- if you do have something to feel guilty about.'

#38 -- Poem is very appropriate for Me w/ Carol.

#39 -- get rid of stress -- get my self esteem up --

#43 -- beware of careful of Linda F. -- We could both get hurt -

#44 --   "   "   "